I Married a Soldier

I Married a Soldier

Lydia Spencer Lane

With an Introduction by Darlis A. Miller

THE UNIVERSITY OF NEW MEXICO PRESS

Albuquerque

Library of Congress Cataloging-in-Publication Data

Lane, Lydia Spencer, 1835–1914.
  I married a soldier.

  Reprint: Originally published: Philadelphia:
Lippincott, 1893.
  Bibliography: p.
  1. Lane, Lydia Spencer, 1835–1914.   2. Frontier and
pioneer life—Southwest, New.   3. Officers' wives—
Southwest, New—Biography.   4. United States.   Army—
Military life.   5. Southwest, New—History—1848–
I. Title.
F786.L3   1987   979′02′0924   87–5035
ISBN 0–8263–0934–8 (pbk.)

First published in 1893.
I Married a Soldier: Old Days in the Old Army © 1964, Horn & Wallace,
Albuquerque, NM Library of Congress No. 64-23617. Introduction ©
1987, The University of New Mexico Press. All rights reserved.

Second printing, 1988.

LYDIA SPENCER LANE traveled to the Southwest as a young army bride, equally inexperienced in the tasks of homemaking and overland traveling. She had married a young lieutenant, William Bartlett Lane, on May 18, 1854 in Carlisle, Pennsylvania, a military town where her family resided. For the next fifteen years, Lydia and William lived a peripatetic life on the western frontier, he as an officer in the United States army and she as a strong-willed officer's wife.

At the time of their marriage, the Southwest had been part of the United States for less than a decade. Among the most prominent symbols of American sovereignty were the military forts erected to protect citizens against Indian depredations. Throughout the West, American Indians resisted encroachment on land they considered their own, making travel exceedingly dangerous for the unwary. Partly as a result of Indian hostility, New Mexico and west Texas remained thinly populated, with small Hispanic settlements clinging to fertile areas along the Rio Grande and other rivers and streams. Only a small fraction of the citizenry was Anglo-American, most having recently arrived as merchants, investors, or government officials over the Santa Fe Trail. The first American woman to cross the prairies to Santa Fe was Susan Shelby Magoffin, who made the trip the summer of 1846. Only a handful of Anglo-American women followed Magoffin in the 1850s, arriving in New Mexico as wives of traders, missionaries, and army officers.

Col. Joseph K. F. Mansfield reported in 1853 that only six "American women" resided in Santa Fe.[1] Lydia Lane, then, who arrived in Santa Fe three years later, was among the first Anglo-American women to experience garrison life in New Mexico.

Many women who followed their officer-husbands west recorded their experiences in diaries, letters to families and friends, and in reminiscences written long after husbands had left the army. At least eleven book-length accounts were published between 1858 and 1910, beginning with Teresa Griffin Vielé's *"Following the Drum": A Glimpse of Frontier Life* (1858).[2] Of the army women who wrote of their experiences in New Mexico, Lydia Lane was among the first to find a publisher. The prestigious Philadelphia firm of J. B. Lippincott published *I Married a Soldier* in 1893. The following year Frances Boyd's *Cavalry Life in Tent and Field* appeared in print. These accounts were followed in the twentieth century with publication of the memoirs and diaries of Marian Sloan Russell, Alice Blackwood Baldwin, and Eveline M. Alexander. The authors shared a curiosity about the West and its people, and their observations help us better understand life and society in territorial New Mexico.[3]

Lydia Spencer Lane's *I Married a Soldier* recounts her life as an officer's wife between 1854 and 1870, years that witnessed a devastating civil war and increased hostility among western Indian tribes. Lydia accompanied her husband on each of his new assignments, and together they made a home for themselves, and, eventually, their three children at military garrisons in Texas and New Mexico. Never staying more than six months at any one post, Lydia fell in love with the army and in her book provides an intimate account of everyday life at several frontier garrisons.

William Bartlett Lane, a native of Kentucky, joined the

Mounted Rifles as a non-commissioned officer in July 1846. He saw action in the Mexican War both at Vera Cruz, where he was wounded, and in Mexico City. Commissioned a second lieutenant in October 1848, he later served at military installations in Kentucky, Missouri, Louisiana, Oregon, and Texas before being posted to Carlisle Barracks in the fall of 1852, where he must have met Lydia. He was promoted to first lieutenant in 1853 and to captain in 1861, about the time his regiment was redesignated the Third Cavalry. His promotion to major came in 1866. For service in connection with disbanding the volunteer army of the United States, he was awarded a brevet lieutenant colonelcy in November 1865. Ill health forced him to retire from the army on December 15, 1870. He died at Fort Monroe, Virginia on June 28, 1898 at about age seventy-two.[4]

In her memoirs, Lydia Lane reveals very little about her own origins, noting only that she was the youngest daughter of Major George Blaney, U.S. Engineer Corps, and that she had a brother living in St. Louis and a sister who married into the army. Though she mentions the birth of each of her three children, Lane reveals the name of only the oldest, Minnie, born at Fort Clark, Texas, in 1855. We do know, however, that Lydia was born about 1835, the same year her father died, and that she was approximately nineteen years old when she married William.[5] Her mother, Mary Elizabeth Biddle Blaney, came from a prominent and wealthy Carlisle family with connections to the Philadelphia Biddles and the Penrose family. Lydia was named after her maternal grandmother, Lydia Spencer Biddle, as were four of her cousins who also carried the name Lydia Spencer.[6]

Shortly after their wedding, William was ordered to join his regiment in Texas, and they arrived at Corpus Christi during a yellow fever epidemic. The overland trip to Fort

Inge, Texas, one of a handful of posts guarding the San Antonio–El Paso road, was a new experience for Lydia, "not at all unpleasant" (p. 27). Thus, Lane allows readers a glimpse of both the good and bad in army life, as she does throughout the book. Though her stay at Fort Inge was brief, she received a good introduction to garrison life. The post itself was dilapidated, with quarters built of logs ready to tumble down. William's pay was barely sufficient to cover the expense of entertaining guests passing from one post to another—a frequent obligation of officers assigned to isolated posts. Wild game and fish supplemented army rations, but Lydia found the companionship of other women limited to the commanding officer's wife.

In the spring of 1855, Lieutenant Lane was ordered to Fort Clark, forty miles northwest of Fort Inge, where in the fall Lydia gave birth to her first child, Mary (or Minnie, as she was called). Though living quarters were primitive, Lydia found Fort Clark to be "a pleasant post," for the garrison included a large number of "officers and ladies" (p. 37). The Lanes moved frequently in 1856—first to San Antonio, a military supply center of a few thousand inhabitants, then to Fort McIntosh in the sun-drenched lower Rio Grande Valley, and finally to New Mexico, where the lieutenant would serve at several frontier posts.

A good storyteller, Lydia conveys in her book the fear, excitement, and discomfort that accompanied her travels in the army. On the march to New Mexico, she was constantly on the lookout for Indians, and she shared with soldiers the effects of the debilitating heat of the desert sun and the enervating chill of a late summer rain storm. William's first station in New Mexico was at Cantonment Burgwin near Taos, but after three weeks there he was ordered to Hatch's

Ranch, about thirty miles south of Las Vegas, New Mexico, where Capt. Washington L. Elliott, Lydia's brother-in-law, would be in command. Though the ranch was isolated and the garrison small, Lydia was delighted to have the company of her sister Valeria, and the two families "passed a very quiet, though pleasant, winter" together (p. 53). In the spring of 1857, Captain Elliot and Lieutenant Lane were ordered to Fort Union, and from there in July Lydia traveled east with her baby to visit relatives in Carlisle.

Lydia remained east for about a year. After a slow, tedious journey across the plains by ox-drawn wagon, she rejoined her husband in November 1858 at Fort Stanton, New Mexico, a beautiful post, according to Lydia, but so isolated that "it was like being buried alive to stay there" (p. 64). Like hundreds of other army wives stationed in far away places, Lane adjusted to the hardships and found pleasure in the congenial society that she helped to create. In May of the following year, William was ordered to Fort Bliss, Texas, which Lydia described as "the most delightful station we had" (p. 68). Even though the garrison was small, the Lanes enjoyed exchanging social visits with civilians living nearby.

Whenever possible, military families like the Lanes employed servants or enlisted men to help with household chores and the care of children. Some families hired Hispanic women as cooks and servants, and others brought with them either white or black domestics from eastern and southern states. Lydia wrote sparingly about the servants she employed, commenting upon the inadequacies of some and praising the loyalty and industry of others. She expressed gratitude for the faithful service performed by several black servants. But she was not without prejudices. In writing about her sister's "servants," a slave family that sought to free themselves at Fort Bliss by crossing the Rio Grande into Mexico, Lane reflected an insensitivity for the plight of slaves that was common among many people of her day.

Lydia's second daughter Susan was born at Fort Bliss in 1859, only a few months before the Lanes set out in October for a visit to Carlisle, traveling by way of San Antonio, Galveston, and New Orleans. They had anticipated a whole year's leave, but William was ordered back to New Mexico the next summer. This would be Lydia's third trip across the plains, and she thoroughly enjoyed it, even though the scenery was monotonous and the days so hot that they left camp at 3 A.M. to take advantage of cool mornings. The Lanes reached Fort Union in September 1860, but by late December they were in Santa Fe enroute to Fort Craig. Conversation on Christmas day focused on the possibility of war between North and South, with advocates for both sides voicing opinions. But, far from the strident voices of disunion, Lydia and her friends had little fear "that matters would ever terminate seriously, and war result" (p. 92). They were mistaken. Like thousands of other American families, the Lanes were soon caught up in the nation's most deadly war.

The author's account of events preceding the Confederate invasion of the Mesilla Valley broadens our understanding of those troublesome times. In February 1861 Lieutenant Lane was ordered to take command of the small garrison at Fort Fillmore, less than twenty miles from the Texas–New Mexico border. Southern sympathizers resided in nearby towns, and Lydia recalled that an "undercurrent of disquiet" surrounded the post (p. 100). Briefly, while William and the troops were away on an aborted Indian scout, Lydia was left in command, having custody of public funds and receiving the daily report of the sergeant of the guard. After fighting broke out in the East, all kinds of rumors circulated in New Mexico of impending Confederate attacks. With considerable success, the author evokes the fear and uncertainty that accompanied the Lanes' departure from Fort Fillmore only hours before Lt. Col. John R. Baylor's force of Texas volunteers entered the area.

Lydia and the children left the territory before the Confederates mounted their campaign into northern New Mexico. They traveled east in the fall of 1861 with a military caravan that included the disgraced Major Isaac Lynde and the paroled troops that had surrendered to Baylor. Lydia long remembered this crossing of the plains, for two weeks before reaching Fort Leavenworth a grass-fire swept through camp, destroying most of their clothing and camping gear. To Lane's surprise, she found her husband awaiting her in Pennsylvania. William had left New Mexico in an overland stage to seek command of a Kentucky regiment and had arrived weeks before his family. Denied his request, William spent the remainder of the war as chief mustering and disbursing officer in Pennsylvania. For his wartime work, he received a brevet appointment as lieutenant colonel, which permitted Lydia and others to call him Colonel Lane.

The Lanes returned to New Mexico the summer of 1866, their family enlarged by the addition of a baby boy. Six new army brides crossed the plains in their party, and the author obviously enjoyed her role as a seasoned campaigner. William's new assignment was in Santa Fe as commander of Fort Marcy, where the Lanes gratefully secured the services of two army physicians for their seriously ill baby. Lydia soon settled into the routine of housekeeping and grew fond of Santa Fe. But in January 1867 the Lanes were again on the move; William was ordered to take command at Fort Union, the largest military installation in New Mexico. The new,

eight-room house assigned to them was but one example of
the poor quality of army construction of that era. When the
plaster dried, the ceilings fell—on one occasion, while Lydia
was preparing dinner for a family of seventeen. Even with
servants, the author found entertaining guests as wife of the
commanding officer an expensive and time-consuming task.
During her years with the army, however, she met and entertained some of the most important people in the territory, including the legendary Kit Carson, of whom she ob-
served: "I never met a plainer, more unpretentious man in
my life." (p. 148).

When Colonel Lane's health declined in the summer of
1867, the Lanes left New Mexico on the advice of a physician, and they spent the next year in the East. After placing their oldest daughter in school, the Lanes started their
return trip in November 1868, traveling by way of New
Orleans, Galveston, and San Antonio. Sometime in March
of the following year they reached Fort Selden, New Mexico,
a new post a few miles north of the abandoned Fort Fillmore, where Lane took command. The family moved into
unfinished quarters, and Lydia was soon busy making butter
and raising chickens. At the end of four months, William's
health was failing so rapidly that a physician advised him to
leave the territory at once. And so they left New Mexico in
the fall. As it turned out, they also left the army and its tran-
sient life-style, much to Lydia's regret. She had thrived on
the challenges of army life, and life as a civilian must have
seemed tame in comparison. More than twenty years later,
Lydia recalled: "Colonel Lane was retired from active service in 1870, to my great grief" (p. 190).

Like reminiscences of other officers' wives, Lane's *I Married a Soldier* focuses on the domestic side of army life. Lane
reminds us that women were very much a part of the military frontier and that families formed a significant element

in the unique society that developed at western garrisons. Marriage and kinship ties were as important in the officer corps as they were in civilian life, offering the possibility of political advancement or preferential treatment as well as strong support in times of adversity.

Not all women ejoyed army life as much as Lane and writers such as Frances Boyd and Eveline Alexander. Their published accounts provide a picture of the frontier army and of the nineteenth-century pioneering experience that balances the harsher view so often portrayed.

I Married a Soldier received favorable review by Capt. Charles King, an army officer turned novelist, in the February 1, 1893 issue of *The Dial.* A second edition of Lane's book was issued in 1910, and the Albuquerque firm of Horn and Wallace reprinted it in 1964 with a new foreword written by Mamie Doud Eisenhower, perhaps the nation's best-known army wife. Lydia Lane, however, has fallen into obscurity, even though her work is often cited in essays and books about the frontier army and western society. Lane was a remarkable woman, sharing several characteristics with other army-women journalists: an eastern upper-middle class background, a good education, and a sharp intelligence. The youngest of three sisters, though the first to marry, Lydia was also high-spirited, which may account for the ease with which she adjusted to the hardships of army life. Like their mother and grandmother before them, Lydia's daughters both married soldiers—Mary to Lt. Joseph L. Garrard in 1883 and Susan to Lt. John F. Guilfoyle in 1887. The Old Army soon passed out of existence, and it was for the younger generation that Lane recorded her reminiscences. Lydia died on June 27, 1914 at about age seventy-nine.[7]

Darlis A. Miller
New Mexico State University

1. Robert W. Frazer, ed., *Mansfield on the Condition of the Western Forts, 1853–54* (Norman: University of Oklahoma Press, 1963), p. 6.

2. Sandra L. Myres, "Introduction," in *Army Letters From an Officer's Wife, 1871–1888* by Frances M. A. Roe (reprint; Lincoln: University of Nebraska Press, 1981), p. ix.

3. See Mrs. Orsemus Bronson Boyd, *Cavalry Life in Tent and Field* (reprint; Lincoln: University of Nebraska Press, 1982); Marian Russell, *Land of Enchantment, Memoirs of Marian Russell Along the Santa Fe Trail as Dictated to Mrs. Hall Russell* (reprint; Albuquerque: University of New Mexico Press, 1981); Robert C. and Eleanor R. Carriker, eds., *An Army Wife on the Frontier: The Memoirs of Alice Blackwood Baldwin, 1867–1877* (Salt Lake City: Tanner Trust Fund, University of Utah Library, 1975); Sandra L. Myres, ed., *Cavalry Wife: The Diary of Eveline M. Alexander, 1866–1867* (College Station: Texas A & M University Press, 1977).

4. Francis B. Heitman, *Historical Register and Dictionary of the United States Army*, vol. 1 (reprint; Urbana: University of Illinois Press, 1965), p. 614. Service and biographical information not found in Heitman was furnished by Dr. Linda J. Lear, Institute for Resources, History and Policy, George Mason University, Fairfax, Virginia.

5. On correspondence dated November 8, 1899, Lydia listed her age as sixty-four. Information courtesy of Dr. Linda J. Lear.

6. Information of Lydia's maternal ancestors, courtesy of Nancy Loughridge, Cumberland County Historical Society, Carlisle, Pennsylvania. Through the Biddle family, Lydia would have been related to Col. James Biddle, whose wife Ellen McGowen Biddle wrote *Reminiscences of a Soldier's Wife,* published by J. B. Lippincott Co. in 1907.

7. Date of death, courtesy of Dr. Linda J. Lear.

I Married a Soldier

PREFACE

IN SENDING FORTH this account of incidents in my army life, I claim for it no literary merit; I have simply given facts without any attempt to elaborate them.

First intended for my children and grandchildren, I afterwards thought this narrative might be acceptable to army friends, and to many of a younger generation who are interested in the old army.

To the former the scenes described may awaken long-forgotten experiences in their own lives; to the latter it will carry the conviction that they will never be called upon to endure what we did.

To-day there is no "frontier;" the wilderness blossoms as the rose; our old deadly enemy, the Indian, is educated, clothed, and almost in his right mind; railroads run hither and yon, and the great trains of army wagons and ambulances are things of the past, whatever civilization may follow.

The hardy, adventurous element in those early pioneer days will ever possess an interest of its own, and I venture to hope that the record of my own experiences will contribute somewhat to the history of those heroic times.

August 18, 1892

ONE

"AND SO THEY were married," and this is how the marriage notice read:

"In Carlisle, Pennsylvania, May 18, 1854 by the Reverend Merwin Johnson, Lieutenant William B. Lane, U.S. Mounted Rifles, and Lydia Spencer, youngest daughter of the late Major George Blaney, U.S. Engineer Corps" (or words to that effect).

The ceremony was short, the marriage feast not elaborate, and after it was over, the farewells spoken amid hearty good wishes for our future happiness, we started for Jefferson Barracks, Missouri, where Lieutenant Lane was to be stationed. Travelling at that time was not as rapid as it is now, and several days passed before we reached the end of our journey; but it was over at last, and, until our quarters were ready (two rooms), we were kindly entertained by Major and Mrs. Charles Ruff, Mounted Rifles. Our housekeeping was on the smallest scale, as we were to remain but a short time at Jefferson Barracks.

We messed with the young officers. It was a sad and anxious summer for us all. Cholera was epidemic, and scarcely a day passed that we did not hear the solemn notes of the "Dead March." Often there were two or three funerals in the twenty-four hours.

The victims were principally among the soldiers. Only two of our friends died: the wife of the late Dr. J. B. Wright, U.S.A., being one of them, and the other, Lieutenant Ferdinand Paine, who was ill but a few hours. He had gone on as officer of the day, in the morning; at midnight he was dead.

Lieutenant Paine had an Indian boy with him, whom he had brought from Oregon. The boy was extremely ill with cholera, and Mr. Paine nursed him faithfully, which, possibly, was the cause of his own illness and death. It required more than a collapsed case of cholera, it seemed, to kill a Digger Indian. He recovered; his master died.

The boy was learning to wait on the table, at the mess. One morning, when he handed me a plate of cakes, I asked if they were hot. He took the shortest way to find out, by laying his hand on top of the pile! "Yes, sir," he said; but I did not take any cakes that morning.

Captain (afterwards Major-General) Hancock and his wife were at Jefferson Barracks that summer. He had just been appointed captain in the Quartermaster's Department. I did not meet him again until after the war, and was much surprised and pleased to find he remembered me; his memory was better than that of some of our old army acquaintances; after they had risen in the world, they "forgot the days of small things."

After a stay of three months at Jefferson Barracks, we packed up our very few worldly possessions and left for the East, making a side trip to Kentucky, *en route* to visit our Southern relatives, and where I knew I would see many things I never saw before; and I did,—different manners and customs, different people, from any I had ever known. How kind and hospitable they all were; how they wanted to entertain us, and give us all they had! Some old family servants walked miles to see "Massa Will's young wife."

We went direct to Carlisle, Pennsylvania, from Kentucky, to await the return of cool weather, when we were to join the regiment, then stationed in Texas. It was unsafe to go South before there was sufficient frost to destroy the germs of yellow fever; but we went too early, after all.

About the middle of October orders were received for Lieutenant Lane to accompany a large party of officers and recruits, going to Texas. So we set off immediately for New York, and joined the command on board the good ship "Middlesex," Captain Parmelee. When I was hoisted up on deck, I found, among other friends, General Sylvester Churchill, who was making an inspection of the ship and troops. The first thing I did was to rush at him, and he ran to me, gathered me up in his arms, and kissed me. When Lieutenant Lane appeared, he was much astonished to see what was going on; though the dear old man had known me always, he had never seen Lieutenant Lane. Explanations followed, introductions were made, and peace in the family was restored.

The ship proved to be an enormous sailing vessel, with ample accommodations for three hundred and sixty recruits,— some having wives and children,—besides several officers and their families. Among the officers were Colonel Sidney Burbank, Captain Ricketts, Zenas R. Bliss, not long out of West Point, I think, Dr. Albert Myer, who was afterwards chief signal-officer of the army, Lieutenant Lane and myself, and possibly others whom I have forgotten.

We sailed away bravely from New York, but one by one we left the deck, so roughly did old Neptune treat us.

Most of us were lost to view before the land was out of sight. It was Saturday when we hoisted sail, and not until the following Thursday did I again appear at table; the weather was rough and stormy, and—well, we had not much appetite. I found things in our state-room in dreadful confusion when I was well enough to look after our belongings. A huge bundle of Bibles had been stored under the lower berth, for what purpose I never knew, unless for distribution among the *Texas heathen*. My travelling-bag and a large bottle of wonderful hair-tonic were there, too, besides a quantity of candy for the voyage, and various other articles. Imagine all these things mixed together in a mass,—cork out of the bottle, candy melted by the contents of it, and the soft, sticky stuff spread over everything. The Bibles had broken bounds, and were in the thickest of it. With the assistance of the stewardess the *débris* was soon cleared away, and order restored.

THE DAYS ON board ship were often tedious, especially along the Florida coast, where we were becalmed for some days, and the heat was very great. The big ship lay almost help-less on the quiet waters, only rising and falling with the ocean swell, but no headway was made. We had become well ac-quainted with our travelling companions by that time, and we, with Dr. Myer and Mr. Bliss, being the youngest of the party, naturally drew close together; hours we passed talking of home and our future, forming a friendship which we thought would be life-long; but Zenas R. Bliss I have never seen since, and Dr. Myer became a great man, and forgot us, I suppose. I have still a small sketch of Hole-in-the-wall, on Abaco Island, drawn for me by Dr. Myer. As well as we could see from the ship, there was an immense hole in a rock, through which the water dashed with great violence. We also saw numbers of enormous green turtle, sunning themselves on the beach of the small is-lands in our course. Looking over the side of the vessel, I noticed masses of what I took to be rock, and was much alarmed, expecting the ship would be dashed to pieces; but my fears were allayed when told it was only sponge that I saw in the clear, green water.

The monotony of the voyage was broken occasionally by the appearance of numerous little boats from the islands near by, manned by the natives, who had fruit, shells, and various curiosities for sale, and which they urged us to buy. We did invest in some very large sea-shells, never dreaming they were inhabited. A few days after we bought them a dreadful odor came from the shells, and there was a burial at sea immediately. The occupant, deprived of his native element, died within his dainty pink walls, and was returned, though too late to benefit him, to the briny deep.

But one death occurred on board the ship, and it was a soldier's child, almost a baby, that was taken. Every one was present on deck when the short funeral services were read over the little body, which had been securely wrapped in canvas and heavily weighted, that it might sink instantly when consigned to the watery grave.

When all was ready, the remains were placed on a board, which was gradually slanted until the little white bundle slowly and surely approached the end of it. Finally, with a dull splash, all that was mortal of the poor baby disappeared in the quiet waters and was seen no more. The mother's agony was heart-rending, as she saw the ocean close over her darling, leaving no trace behind.

We had been out from New York two weeks when we sighted the coast of Texas, but, as the weather was dark and tempestuous, the captain put back to sea, and it was several days before we again reached Aransas Pass. Arriving there, we left the big ship which had carried us safely through the troubled waters. We were sorry to part with Captain Parmelee, who had done everything possible to make the voyage agreeable and comfortable. From the ship we were transferred to the "Josephine," an old steamboat well known to army people long ago. Before leaving the "Middlesex," the captain gave me a St. Bernard puppy of almost pure breed, the mother and her litter coming with us on the ship from New York. He was a beauty,—jet black, with a white star on his forehead,—and we named him Parmelee, which we shortened, calling him Lee.

Our voyage on the "Josephine" was not a long one, which we did not regret. While walking about the boat and looking around, I noticed, on the lower deck, a very much coiled and speckled mass, that attracted my attention immediately. I called the captain, and pointed it out, asking what it was. His answer was a cry of horror, and he yelled for "Tom, Jim, John, to come out with spades, axes, shovels, to kill that moccasin." It was one of the most poisonous snakes in that region, and its presence there was unaccountable.

From the "Josephine," we were taken on to a "lighter,"—a small schooner, I would call it,—which was to carry us to Corpus Christi. There was only room on it for a few of the officers, Colonel Burbank and family, Lieutenant Lane and myself. Other transportation was provided for the soldiers, baggage, etc.

We passed the night on the "lighter." I cannot say we slept. The accommodations were of the most contracted description, there being scarcely room to stand upright in the hold, where Mrs. Burbank, children, nurse, and myself were stowed away. We improved our time fighting roaches and other things, down below, while the officers spent the night on deck. We made the best of the situation, and had a very funny time, astonishing our friends above us with many a hearty laugh. They wondered what we found down in the depths to amuse us so much.

Our breakfast next morning was not luxurious,—bread, very good, without butter, fried bacon, and coffee, but no milk. We were hungry, and accepted the simple fare most thankfully.

We were to reach Corpus Christi about noon that day. By some means we heard, before we landed, that people were dying on every side from yellow fever. There had been no frost up to that time in Texas. Notwithstanding, the troops were sent down from the North, regardless of the risk they ran, right into the midst of the epidemic then raging, and with a fair prospect of dying by hundreds from it.

It was dreadful news to us, as there was no escape, no running away from it, nothing to do but land, take the risk, and trust in Providence. However, I had "gone for a soldier," and a soldier I determined to be.

We found our camp ready for us, right on the beach, at Corpus Christi,—tents pitched for officers and men. They were selected according to rank. By the time the young officers' turn came to secure one, it was Hobson's choice,—take what was left, or nothing. I heard, afterwards, a wall-tent had been pitched and floored for us especially; but we only saw the outside of it. An unmarried officer, who had more rank than Lieutenant Lane, and an eye to comfort, appropriated it immediately.

We were put into a large hospital-tent, with an opening at each end, which could be closed when necessary. We had no board-floor in it, and only the sands of the sea for carpeting.

I went into the tent with a heavy heart, for I expected nothing less than an outbreak of yellow fever in the camp. Indeed, the situation was grave enough to alarm any one; but the very first night we spent ashore a violent norther struck the coast, and the weather became very cold. A heavy frost was the result, and not another case of fever was reported in the town; but many of those then ill died, in consequence of the sudden change in the temperature.

We were very happy, of course, having escaped the awful disease, and began cheerfully to make preparations for the march we had before us to Fort Inge, Texas, to which post Lieutenant Lane had been assigned.

One night, during the norther, the wind blew a hurricane, and our tent was torn open at both ends. Between the pounding of the waves on the beach, the shrieking of the wind, and the flapping of the canvas, the noise was fearful; and I expected to be blown bodily out to sea. With the assistance of some soldiers, after a violent struggle, the tent was made secure, and we managed to live in our uncomfortable quarters until we left Corpus Christi.

THREE

WE HAD AN Irishman, who had gone with us from Carlisle; very honest and good, though entirely green as to any knowledge of cooking; but really not much more so than I was, in those early days, and I was to teach him what I did not know myself! We went to work together, to cook the meals, which, necessarily, were of the simplest description.

I knew how things ought to look and taste, but did not understand just how to prepare them. For a time, I believe, we were obliged to eat soldiers' rations,—only hard tack, fried salt pork, and coffee without milk, and I honestly tried to enjoy them, set out as they were on top of the mess-chest. An empty candle-box and a bucket turned upside down, served as seats round this humble board, until we could get into the village, to make a few purchases of such articles as we needed to take up the country with us. We found in the shops what answered very well for army life at that remote period; but a second lieutenant nowadays would not consider our best things sufficiently good for his kitchen.

Transportation was very limited, and we were only allowed room enough for articles absolutely necessary. The bachelor officers often came to the relief of married men, giving up the space in a wagon to which they were entitled for their use, so that we generally found a place for all we wanted to carry.

Those were the days before railroads were even dreamed of in that far-away country. Everything was carried from the coast of Texas in wagons drawn by mules or oxen. Strangers arriving at Galveston, Indianola, or Corpus Christi had not much choice in the matter of conveyance for continuing their journey into the interior of the country. An ambulance, a horse, or a mule made up the assortment, and if he could not decide on one of these modes of travel, he must walk, or stay where he was. Some of those obliged to remain would almost have been willing to walk, for the sake of getting away from those little towns, as they were then.

All preparations were at last made for our march, the orders given to pack wagons and strike tents. An ambulance was provided for the ladies and children,—only one,—where, I was sorry to find, I was to ride daily. Many a weary hour I passed in it, with only space enough to sit bolt upright, when I was not diving under the seat for the family lunchbox, which was brought out six or eight times a day for the children. The mother and nurse were stout, and it was a serious matter for either to get down on the floor and drag out the box. I was young and slender, and was not supposed to have any objection to jumping up and down, whenever the children said they were hungry. I did object, but behaved very well, and tried to look amiable.

We travelled from Corpus Christi to the western frontier through a dreary, desolate country, where nothing lived but Indians, snakes, and other venomous reptiles, and I expected to see some dreadful thing whichever way I turned. I never went to bed without making a thorough search for a snake, tarantula, or centipede; but in all the years I spent travelling and camping, I never saw a snake about the tents, and very few poisonous insects, either, so that, as time went on, and I did not find the thing for which I watched, I grew careless, but not on that first expedition, where all was so new to me.

By the time we left Corpus Christi the St. Bernard puppy was growing fast, and, of course, with his cunning ways, was a great pet with everybody. He was put into our wagon, on leaving camp, where there was some one to look after him. But one day the watchman went to sleep, and our poor puppy crawled out of the wagon, fell under the wheels, and was killed instantly. There were great sorrow and indignation in the camp when it was known Lee was dead, and the soldiers who pitched our tents would not allow the man who had charge of him to come about the place. I cried all day for my puppy, and never would have another.

Mike, the Irishman, and I were beginning to know something of cooking by this time. The viands were of the plainest. We did not attempt any dish that required much skill to prepare. As we had nothing in the way of bread but hard-tack, we learned to make biscuit. Our first effort was a failure,—spoiled in the baking. We had only a "Dutch oven" in which to cook bread or meat, and experience was absolutely necessary to know just how hot to make it. Mike burned the first batch to a coal, turned it over, and baked the other side. Nothing daunted, I kept on until, between us, we could make most excellent pounded biscuit.

After the camp was in order for the evening, and supper over, Mike carefully washed off the top of the mess-chest inside, and I made biscuit for the next day. When the dough was prepared, I pounded it well with a long-necked bottle, the neck serving as a handle, which answered the purpose very well.

Often, while the bread-making was going on, we were joined round the camp-fire by Dr. Myer and Mr. Bliss, and many a hot biscuit they ate, with molasses, from a tin plate. Judging from the rapidity with which the biscuits disappeared, they must have been very good, indeed. I wonder if Colonel Bliss (it is now) would remember those evenings beside the camp-fire? Many years after, I met General Myer in Washington, and discovering, in a few moments, how very short his memory was, I brought up some incidents of the journey, such things as no one would likely forget. I asked if he recollected how he and Mr. Bliss ate hot biscuit and molasses. His reply was that he "remembered the march, but not the biscuit and molasses." Poor man! he is dead now.

We travelled along very slowly, but, to most of us, it was a new experience, and not at all unpleasant.

We were glad when we approached Fort McIntosh, Texas, for several officers of the Mounted Rifles were stationed there, and we were sure of a hearty welcome and hospitable entertainment. The day we were expected at the post, several of the officers rode out to meet us,—W. L. Elliott and Roger Jones among them,—and greeted us warmly. We were driven at once to the house of the commanding officer, W. W. Loring, colonel Mounted Rifles.

Captain W. L. Elliott (afterwards major-general) and Lieutenant Roger Jones (afterwards inspector-general of the army) messed with Colonel Loring, and we enjoyed our few days' visit to them very much. I was treated with great consideration, being the youngest and latest bride in the regiment. The change from camp life and camp fare was extremely pleasant to us, and we would have liked to remain longer than we did. It would also have been agreeable to our friends, I think, to have us with them. It was seldom any one came to their isolated post. No one travelled in that direction for amusement in those days. Nothing but stern necessity and duty took people to such a desolate place, so, when strangers did arrive, they were kindly welcomed and entertained.

FOUR

I WAS MUCH pleased when our kind friends at Fort Mc-Intosh told me that, when we left, I should have an ambulance for myself; so I was perfectly independent in future, and had all the room I wanted. They did not forget, either, to put into it many tokens of remembrance, such as luncheon, champagne, books, etc.

We said good-by with much regret, when the day came to leave, everybody had been so hospitable and kind, not only to us, but to all the officers in the party.

The march was resumed in the same deliberate way; the soldiers were on foot, and we had to keep pace with them; hours and hours we were, making the daily distance of ten or fifteen miles between camps. We halted frequently to rest the men and mules, and then the ladies and children would gladly get out of the ambulances, and perhaps walk along the road for a change; but we dared not get away from the command. It was certain the Indians were never far off, and we kept very close to the soldiers.

In due course of time we reached Fort Duncan, on the Rio Grande. It was a wretched place to live in, and I am sure some of our companions who were to remain there looked on their future station with sinking hearts when they saw it for the first time.

Lieutenant R. W. Johnson took charge of us, and had a tent pitched for our use in his yard, not having a spare room in their house. We took our meals with them, which was a real treat. He and Mrs. Johnson made us very comfortable for two or three days before we started for our own station, Fort Inge.

R. W. Johnson is now retired as major-general U.S. Army, and is a wealthy resident of St. Paul, Minnesota. I met him quite recently, and he had not forgotten our visit to Fort Duncan, so long ago.

One of the officers stationed at Fort Duncan at that time was Abner Doubleday; his wife was with him, a pretty, refined woman, and she was more afraid of a mouse than anything in the world. I remember she had a frame fixed all around her bed and covered with netting to keep them out. She did not seem to dread snakes at all, nothing but an awful mouse!

All those with whom we had travelled from "the States" remained at Fort Duncan, to their regret. We parted from our friends sorrowfully, and with an escort of soldiers left for Fort Inge.

During the first day's travel we came across a camp, where we found some old friends and dined with them. They were Captain and Mrs. McLean; she was Margaret, daughter of General E. V. Sumner, U.S. Army. They were comfortably fixed in tents, and seemed satisfied.

Quite a curious thing had happened to her, just before we met. The tents had shelters made of branches of trees (or bushes), to keep off the sun, built over and around them, which extended out like a porch, making a pleasant shade. Mrs. McLean was sitting sewing one day, with her back to the shelter, and as she drew out her needle her hand came close to the brush, when a snake darted out and bit it. Naturally, they were much alarmed; but the proper remedies were applied at once, and no bad results followed. She sat farther away next time.

We were three or four days, if I am not mistaken, going from Fort Duncan to Fort Inge, and were glad to reach the

place, forlorn as it was. The post was dilapidated; but the surroundings were far more agreeable than at either Fort McIntosh or Fort Duncan. A beautiful little river, the Leona, ran
just behind the quarters, which were built of logs, and almost
ready to tumble down. We moved into a vacant house of four
rooms; the kitchen was behind it, and was in an advanced stage
of decay. A high wind might easily have blown it over.

Our supply of furniture was not sufficient even for four
rooms. We had taken out with us two carpets, and enough
pretty chintz for curtains in two rooms; six hard (*so hard!*)
wooden chairs, bought in Corpus Christi, and called "Windsor
chairs,"—why, I don't know,—a bedstead, centre-table, a cook-
ing-stove, which was about the most valuable and highly prized
of all our possessions, and a few other articles of the plainest
description. We were well provided with good china, glass,
house-linen, and silver. We had all we wanted, and were very
happy.

The pay per month for a first lieutenant of Mounted Rifles
was ninety-three dollars!—vast wealth, it seemed to me. More
would have been useless, for there was nothing to buy,—no
stores nearer than San Antonio,—so that the commissary bill
was the only one we owed monthly, except servants' wages and
one to the laundress, and we saved money. The commissary
furnished only necessary articles of food at that time, such as,
coffee, flour, sugar, rice, ham, and pork, which list of eatables
did not offer much to tempt the appetite; the day of canned
meats, vegetables, and fruits was not yet.

Butter, eggs, and chickens were brought to the post sometimes from the ranches, eighteen or twenty miles away, the
owners running the risk of being murdered by the Indians
every trip they made.

Game was very abundant, and almost at our door; deer,
turkeys, partridges, and ducks could be found right round the

post, while the lovely clear stream that ran just back of the house was filled with magnificent black bass, which were easily caught.

Behind the quarters, and extending to the river, was a grove of fine old live-oak trees, and many an hour we passed fishing under their shade, I for minnows to bait the hooks for bass; and in a few minutes I caught enough to supply the fishermen, who only condescended to catch the game fish in a scientific manner, with rod and reel. Fine sport they had, the bass taken often weighing six and eight pounds.

We became very tired of all the fine game, and would have welcomed a good beef-steak as a luxury. There were so few soldiers at the post that beef was issued only once or twice a month, and was really a treat.

It was fortunate for us there was such a supply of game, for, almost from the day we began housekeeping, we had guests to entertain,—people passing from one post to another,—and we had more than our share of them. When meat was not to be had, an hour's fishing and hunting gave us all we required. We had no vegetables except rice, hominy, and beans. Macaroni was a stand-by, but we had to send to San Antonio for it.

Mike, with the help of my old family receipts, had become quite a good plain cook, and was kept busy with our numerous guests. The first one on the list was a Texas Ranger, Captain Walker. I suppose he was a militia-man, employed by the government to look after Indians on the Western frontier.

Our little centre-table was the only one we had, and did not answer very well for three people to sit at and hold the various dishes at dinner; some rested on the floor, others on chairs, but this did not have the least effect on the captain's healthy appetite. It was all we could do, so we did not apologize.

We became very weary of entertaining people of whom we knew nothing; but there was no hotel nor house of any kind where they could go, so the officers felt themselves obliged to look after their comfort and take them in.

I remember one very cold night, at Fort Inge, we heard the rattle of an ambulance coming into the garrison, then stop at our house. First an elderly woman stepped out, then a fat man, followed by two young men. As no one came forward to help us entertain these citizens, we had to do the best we could for them. We were only able to provide a bed for the old couple, and the young men slept in the ambulance.

Our supply of bedding was very limited, outside of what we needed for ourselves. Our only mattress, pillows, and blankets were laid on the parlor floor for the lady and her husband, while we shivered all night on a straw under-bed and such miscellaneous covers as we could gather up. We gave our visitors all we had, but I do not think they ever felt grateful for what we did. They almost ruined our best carpet, during their stay, by spilling something on it, and trying to wash out the stain. We never saw them after they left, and did not remember their enforced visit with much pleasure. We had the honor, that winter, of entertaining a young German baron. He certainly did not return to the Fatherland with the idea that the officers of the United States Army lived very luxuriously, after staying at our quarters and dining at our frugal board.

Fort Inge was a one-company post, commanded by Captain Thomas Duncan, Mounted Rifles. Later in the winter, Colonel George B. Crittenden, Mounted Rifles, took command, and Doctor Howard, of San Antonio, was sent to look after the sick. Mrs. Duncan and myself were the only ladies at the post.

IN FEBRUARY HUSBAND was granted a short leave of absence, and we made a visit to San Antonio, and Austin, where Dr. R. N. Lane, my brother-in-law, was practising medicine, and well known to many army people.

We left Fort Inge in an ambulance, with no escort; Mr. Lane and the driver were supposed to be a sufficient guard through a country where there were some small settlements and a house to sleep in every night.

At the end of the first day's ride, we found Dhanis, a small German settlement, where one Mr. Finger kept a house for wayfarers. The ladies' bedroom—there seemed to be but one— was small, with a low ceiling, stone floor, and large, open fireplace. The furniture consisted of a bed, wash-stand, some extremely uncomfortable chairs, and a small table, on which our meals were served. With a big fire of dry logs, we felt quite content, after being in the cold wind all day. The fare was simple, but not bad, and, with healthy appetites, we enjoyed the novelty of the situation.

In all my wanderings I have never come across another such bed as that! It was shaped just like an egg, and we had to cling like bats to stay in it at all, and had very little rest. I am sure Mr. Finger would have been surprised had we told him the bed was uncomfortable. The ladies' chamber was, I think, the pride of the house. Men were put to sleep in a room that opened into the stable, and an army officer told me he awoke suddenly one morning, and, on looking up, saw a horse's head just above his own.

The next stop we made was at Castroville, where we found quite a nice house kept by a quaint old French woman,— Madam Tardee,—well patronized by army people at that time. The house was clean, and the fare better than one would expect. The bedrooms, up-stairs, were divided by canvas partitions, and we had to whisper if we did not want to be heard all over the house. Later on we found canvas played a conspicuous part in the building of Texas houses. Sometimes one whole side would be made of it, the occupants intending, "some day," to replace it with more substantial material.

On the third day we drove into San Antonio, stopping at the Plaza House, then the best hotel in the town. It was on the main Plaza, not far from the Cathedral. San Antonio was more Mexican than American then, and the foreign style of architecture interested me very much; also the gardens, filled as they were with tropical trees and unfamiliar plants and flowers.

After resting at San Antonio, we drove to Austin, taking three or four days to make the distance. We found some very pleasant, cultivated people at Austin, among them Miss Annie Swisher, whom Dr. Lane eventually married; a brighter woman I never met anywhere. Tom Ochiltree, the celebrated, was at that time an Austin society-man.

In two weeks our leave was up, and we left for the Western frontier. We travelled two days, without incident or trouble, from San Antonio towards Fort Inge. Though the drive on the third day was long and tedious, we hoped to reach the post soon after dark. The roads were heavy from recent rains; any one at all familiar with the black and sticky Texas mud can understand the meaning of "heavy roads." Evening came upon us when we were still many miles from the fort. The mules showed signs of giving out, and the prospect of reaching home that night was anything but bright.

Husband and the driver held a consultation on the situation; it was certain the mules could travel no farther. The driver thought there was a place not far off the road, where we might be allowed to spend the night; so we turned into a dim path, following it until we came to the house. It was so dark by this time we could scarcely see where we were going; but the door was found at last, and, after thundering on it with tremendous force time and again, a voice called out, "What do you want?" Husband answered, "To stay all night." "You can't do it." "But we must; there is a lady here, our mules are broken down, and we cannot go on." "That makes it worse; having a lady, you can't stay." More parleying followed, when finally a reluctant consent was given for me to go into the house, and the door was opened. As the driver turned the ambulance into the corral, a voice called to him "to be careful, as there was a bit of a bank near," which in the morning we found to be a sheer descent of at least two hundred feet to the river below, and we had gone close to the edge in the night, never dreaming of its vicinity!

We were taken into a small room, where a fire of big logs burned brightly. By the light of it I studied the owner of the voice who had talked in the darkness to us. It was a superb-looking old man I saw, with snow-white beard to his waist. His mild, benevolent face gave me confidence at once, and his manner was kind and gentle.

There were several awkward girls and young men in the room, who were his children, he told us. Without asking permission, the old man mixed me a drink of whiskey and honey, which I declined; but he insisted so much on my tasting it, I did so, rather than hurt his feelings. One of the girls was preparing supper for us, of which we were much in need, and when ready we did full justice to it, simple as it was,—corn-bread, bacon, and coffee, but no butter nor milk.

In the course of the evening, one of the sons, recently

married, came in, leading his bride by the hand. Her appearance was so ludicrous I could not repress a smile. Her frock came about to her knees, and below it appeared pantalettes to her heels. A large sun-bonnet, entirely concealing her face, completed her costume.

When time came to retire, we found we were to share the common sleeping-room of the family, there being no other. Indeed, we were fortunate to have a bed to ourselves! Besides the one given to us were several others, which were filled by two old men, two young men, two girls, and two boys,—ten people in one small room; only three were women, of whom I was one!

There was no sleep for me that night. It turned out the old men had been to a horse-race the day before, and they were going over it in their dreams, shouting and swearing incessantly. My faith in the patriarchal-looking old man was destroyed as I listened to his loud and angry voice while he slept. I lay watching for the dawn, and could plainly see the stars through the cracks in the roof. As they disappeared and morning broke, we got up and made hasty preparations for departure, and, after paying for our night's lodging, we left, very thankful to escape from such a place.

We heard, afterwards, the true character of these people. They were outlaws of the worst description; but while we were under their roof they treated us well.

Shortly before we stayed at their house one of the boys accidentally shot and killed his brother. Throwing down his gun, he exclaimed, "I have the damnedest luck of any fellow I know!"

We were happy to reach Fort Inge and home the next day, and made no more expeditions until we left for Fort Clark.

THE OFFICERS AND SOLDIERS stationed at Fort Inge
were ordered to Fort Clark in the spring, and Inge was abandoned for several years.

Fort Clark was a pleasant post, on the Las Moras River,
within a day's drive of our old station. The change was very
agreeable to us all, the garrison being a large one, with a number of officers and ladies.

A funny little house had been put up for us before we
arrived, all the quarters for officers being occupied. The walls
were built of green logs with the bark left on them, and they
were set up on end,—not like the usual log-cabin. The Mexicans call a house of that kind a "jacal" (pronounced *hackal*).
The walls were seven or eight feet high, and supported a slanting roof. There was really but one room in the house, with an
enormous chimney, built of stone, in the middle of it. The
spaces between the logs were chinked with mud, or plaster,
perhaps, but that was all the plaster there was about it. We had
no ceiling,—nothing but the shingles over our heads through
the long, hot summer. On one side of the big chimney was the
bedroom, on the other, a sitting-room. We had a porch at one
end of the house, with a shelter of bushes to protect us from
the sun, and we had also a room, some distance off, for a kitch-
en, where Mike set up his stove, and we were at housekeeping
again. The kitchen floor was nothing but the ground, so there
was no scrubbing to be done,—it could only be sprinkled and
swept.

In the summer Mike left us to work for the quartermaster. No one could be found to take his place but "French Josephine," a poor exchange, but we were glad to have any one. She gave us very little of her society or anything else, only coming home in time to prepare our very frugal meals. She knew the time of day by the bugle-calls, and often asked me, "Did stable-call *went* yet?"

Our little house was so far from the other quarters, I think the Indians could have crept in upon us, taken our scalps, and ridden away, without being molested. Nothing troubled us, however, but the field-rats and mice, which were there in numbers when we first occupied the house. They came into the room round the walls, where the boards of the floor were scooped out to fit the upright logs of which the house was built. All being green at first, they dried during the intensely hot summer, and very soon the floor and walls were far apart, so that the rats and mice came and went without ceremony. We saw a rat drag a small bottle of sweet-oil from one side of the room all the way across, and down under the floor on the other side.

The rats and mice were bad, but we found a tremendous snake on the mantel-piece, and that was much worse. I was just about to retire one night, when we heard a suspicious rustling among some papers, and there he was, moving cautiously among them; how it ever got up there we could not imagine. I fled out of doors, while husband killed it with his sabre. Another large one was killed in the brush at the end of the porch. Sometimes a skunk would pass the house, but never very close. He is a beautiful little animal *to see*; but distance lends enchantment in his case.

I must not forget to tell of the chicken-coop, built by the "lieutenant," at a great outlay, not of money, but of patience and temper. The material was oak barrel-staves, hard and dry, into which it was almost impossible to drive a nail. The builder started to work in the morning cheerfully, and anxious to complete the job. For a few moments the hammering went on vigorously; then the hatchet could be seen flying through the air into the chaparral. Much time was spent hunting for it, but it seemed a relief to the wounded feelings (or fingers) to send the hatchet spinning into space, when it had come in contact with a thumb or finger. By the time the coop was finished there was not a sound one on either hand.

In the fall our first daughter was born. I had no one to take care of her and me but husband and the doctor. The ladies of the garrison took turns dressing the baby, every day, as I could not trust the French girl to touch her. When she was three days old there was a violent storm, and the rain poured into the house through the crevices between the logs, out of which the plaster had long since fallen. We were covered over with blankets, to keep us dry, and did not suffer at all; but the situation was not pleasant for the mother of a three-days'-old baby. If that poor child had known of how many comforts she was deprived by coming into the world on the Western frontier, she would have been much aggrieved, and, if it were possible, would have yelled louder than she did. My own experience was extremely limited regarding the needs of a young baby; but in after-years I knew the poor thing had been starved and half frozen, in consequence of which she cried for six months, and hardly slept day or night, the only means she had of showing she was badly treated.

The day before Christmas we left Fort Clark for a second visit to San Antonio and Austin. The weather was like summer, and the evening was so warm in camp we were glad to get out of the tent for the air. By morning a stiff norther was blowing, and water in a bucket in the tent froze to the bottom. It was bitter cold, and we were so anxious about the baby, fearing

she might freeze to death. Our ambulance was better calcu-
lated for a summer ride than a journey on a freezing winter's
day. Our driver, Biles by name, had begun very early in the
morning to celebrate Christmas by taking a great deal more
whiskey than was good for him, which he procured from some
unknown source. As it was a warm day when we left Fort
Clark, he, soldier-like, "took no thought for the morrow," and
forgot his overcoat. We found out as soon as we started from
camp that the man was too drunk to drive, and we had not
gone far before he became unconscious. He was propped up on
the front seat beside husband, who drove, and who occasionally
administered a sharp crack over his head with the whip, to
rouse him and keep him from freezing to death. I sat behind,
with the baby on my lap, completely covered with blankets to
protect her from the wind, and many an anxious peep I took to
see how she fared, lest, while keeping her warm and excluding
the cold air, I might smother her.

There we were, travelling over the prairie, far from any settlement, with no escort, and a young baby and a helplessly
drunken soldier to be cared for. It was an anxious day for us,
and we were much relieved when, late in the afternoon, we
could see the little town of Dhanis in the distance, where we
would find a fire and the assistance we needed.

A new house of entertainment had been built since our
last visit. We were given a large, bare-looking, carpetless room,
with an open fireplace, which, from some defect in the chimney, smoked dreadfully, and all the doors and windows had to
be left open in consequence, so that we really regretted old
Finger's guest-chamber, with the stone floor and egg-shaped
bed. Biles recovered by the time we reached the house, and
when the blankets were removed from the baby she was found
to be as cheerful as possible, and seemed to enjoy the numerous
volunteer nurses who came to my relief. One especially she

liked extremely,—a girl with one leg shorter than the other, who held her in her arms and rose on the long leg, and then came down on the short one, all the time making a humming, grunting noise in her throat that seemed to charm the baby. We would have liked to keep her as nurse, but she could not leave her home.

The next day we continued our travels, which were un-eventful to the end. We were tired when we reached Austin, and glad to rest, and we remained some time with our kind friends at their pleasant home.

When we returned to San Antonio, husband, much to our delight (or my delight, at least), was ordered to remain there on duty. We rented a small house, or rather two three-roomed houses together, where we lived until May. There were no communicating doors, so we had to go into the street to reach the sitting-room from our bedroom. The kitchen was by itself, in the yard; but these inconveniences were mere trifles. When we left Austin we took with us two black servants, a cook, and a small girl as nurse, who announced to me that her name was "Miss Indiana Maria Jane Walton;" but whether she adopted the name, or it was given by her sponsors, I do not know. Her resources for amusement were wonderful, and she talked all day to the baby, who seemed to understand and admire her black face very much. She tied strings to the door-mat, put the baby on it, and took her to pay imaginary visits, the mat serv-ing as a carriage, while Miss Walton herself, with long shaving curls hanging from her ears, was horse and chaperon at the same time, looking entirely serious and very important.

SEVEN

IN MAY LIEUTENANT LANE was ordered to proceed to Fort McIntosh, a twelve days' journey from San Antonio by wagon. It is now made in less than that many hours by the cars. We knew what to expect in the way of quarters, etc., as we had been there a few days when travelling from the coast to Fort Inge. The friends whom we left at McIntosh were all gone, and their places filled by strangers, but they received us kindly, and we were soon quite at home.

The heat was dreadful. The houses were mere shells, entirely exposed to the baking sun all day long. Not a green thing was to be seen but a few ragged mesquite-trees. Here and there a blade of grass attempted to grow in the scorching, sandy soil, but it was soon burned up by the hot sun.

Back of our quarters was quite a large yard, but there was not a living thing in it, except tarantulas, scorpions, and centipedes, with an occasional rattlesnake for variety. As long as we left them undisturbed they were harmless. I found a large tarantula by the house one day, and teased it with a stick. He stood up immediately on his great hairy hind legs and showed fight, when I left him to amuse himself with the piece of wood, and got out of his way.

During that summer—1856—the regiment of Mounted Rifles was ordered to New Mexico, and we were soon on the move again, after having been about two months at McIntosh. We left July 16, to join the troops at Fort Clark, from which point they were to begin a march of nearly one thousand miles, which would take them far into the fall to accomplish, being obliged to travel slowly to save the animals as much as possible through the hot weather.

We arrived at Fort Clark on the 22d of July, and remained until the 27th, when, everything being ready, we left with one of the three columns into which the regiment was divided, and which were two or three days' travel apart. We had quite a comfortable "outfit" for a lieutenant and family, owning a pretty little ambulance and as fine a pair of large gray mules as one would wish to see. They could travel all day without—in sporting parlance—"turning a hair." On the first day out from Clark they fully demonstrated there was plenty of life in them. I was sitting on the front seat of the carriage, holding the reins, while husband was on the back one with the baby, when a rider-less horse came rushing by. Away went the lively grays across the prairie, when the baby was quickly deposited on my lap, and a stronger hand than mine seized the reins and brought the frisky fellows round to the road, after a good run and looking none the worse for it.

There were several ladies besides myself with the command, but we saw very little of each other those awful hot days. We broke camp, usually, at daylight every morning, and tents were again pitched at noon, when we had little desire for anything but to get under shelter and stay there until the sun went down. Then, after enjoying the cool breeze, which nearly always came with the night in Texas, we were ready to retire. How well I remember the sweet evening air, laden, as it often was, with the fragrance of a little plant that covered the camp ground, and which bore a tiny yellow flower. As the wagons rolled over and bruised it, the air was filled with the delicious odor, which was the same as the lemon, verbena, or balm. I have often wondered why it was not utilized for making perfumery; perhaps it has been by this time.

Bedtime came early in camp. By ten o'clock, or even before,

lights were out, and nothing could be heard but the tramp of
the sentinel, the rattle of the chains by which the mules were
fastened to the wagons, and the steady munching noise made
by the animals while chewing their corn. Frequently the coyotes came outside the camp and serenaded us with their dreary,
melancholy howls and barks, but we were too weary to be
disturbed by them. All was peaceful, and it was hard to believe
that behind that little rise, or clump of grass, Indians could
easily watch what was going on, and be ready to run off any
stray mule or horse that chanced to wander their way.

There were several army posts along our route, and to arrive at one was a pleasant variety in the irksomeness of the long
days. Camp Lancaster was the first we passed,—August 2,—and
was the worst station I had seen in Texas, but the ladies I met
at the post seemed cheerful and contented. We dined with
Captain and Mrs. R. S. Granger. On the 12th we reached Fort
Davis, where the quarters were bad, but the surroundings very
beautiful. We met with much kindness and hospitality everywhere we stopped, receiving presents of butter, eggs, milk, etc.
No one knows, who has not been deprived of these necessities,
what a luxury a little milk or a pat of butter becomes when unobtainable, which was usually the case with us when travelling.
Often, in Texas, when we tried to buy milk at a ranch, where
there were thousands of cattle, there was not a drop to be had.
The owners would not take the trouble to have it even for
themselves. So you can understand how we enjoyed the numerous dainties sent us by friends as we wandered in the wilds of
Texas.

We made what was called a very quick journey to Fort
Bliss, from Fort Clark, arriving August 27, two days less than a
month on the road. Now, one can be half around the world in
that time, and we had only travelled between five and six hundred miles. Think of it!

When we struck some Mexican towns on the Rio Grande, below Fort Bliss, we were delighted; it was so pleasant to see again green trees and grass, after having had, for so long, nothing but the Spanish bayonet and soap-weed on which to rest our weary eyes.

I was constantly on the lookout for Indians, and a number of bayonet-plants together had given me many a scare, assuming in the distance almost any shape,—men on horseback and on foot. Some of them grow very tall, and the leaves, shaped much like a bayonet, stand out stiff and straight from the top of the tree. When it dies the spike-like leaves turn downward, covering the stalk to the ground. At the top of it the blossoms appear, first coming up in a solid mass, not unlike a conical-shaped cabbage-head. As it grows the flowers come out in rows of white bells, all attached to a thick stem, which is frequently eighteen inches high, perhaps more. The pretty, dainty flowers seem hardly to belong to the stiff, prim-looking tree.

After having been deprived as long as we were of fruit and vegetables, it was delightful to find ourselves just in time for the delicious peaches and grapes, brought fresh from old Mexico, over the Rio Grande, every day to Fort Bliss. I spent hours over the camp-fire, in the broiling sun, preserving peaches for future use. I never enjoyed anything more in my life than those twelve days in our pretty camp on the Rio Grande, at Fort Bliss, and was so sorry when the orders said "move on." We laid in what fruit we could carry, chickens, etc., for the rest of the march. We had coops for the chickens, which were tied on behind the wagons, and after reaching camp the doors were opened and the poor things turned out. They never left the wagons, but went to roost on them at night, where they were caught and put back into the coops for an early start next day.

Fort Fillmore, on the Rio Grande, was forty miles from Fort Bliss, and in New Mexico. Such a dreary-looking place I

have seldom seen; but there were some Mexican settlements
only a few miles off, which were quite accessible, and when the
officers and ladies were tired of home they could go to see their
Mexican neighbors. We stayed there part of a day to have the
ambulance repaired, and dined with Lieutenant and Mrs.
John D. Wilkins.

At Fort Thorn we found some of the regiment in quarters,
having been ordered to remain. We were delighted it was not
to be our station, and were glad to leave. We remained in camp
at the post for some time, awaiting orders. Near us were several
dragoon companies ("troops," nowadays) in camp, and among
the officers we found some old friends, "Old Billy Grier" for
one, whom everybody in the army knew and liked.

Our next move was towards Fort Craig. We camped one
night on ground covered with grease-wood, the roots of which
are quite large and burn well, though too rapidly for comfort;
it was all the fuel we had. A severe storm of wind and rain set
in that night, and by morning it was so cold I tried to stay in
bed with the baby to keep warm. It was decided not to move
that day, hoping by the next the weather would be clear. The
baby was rather a restless young person to be shut up with in a
tent, on a cold, rainy day. She did not approve at all of keeping
under the covers, so we had sheet-iron pans filled with hot coals
and ashes put into the tent to heat it, and, rolling up in shawls,
we got up and were quite comfortable. All day, and the night
following, the floods came down, and husband concluded to
move camp next morning. There was still no sign of clearing
weather. We started ahead of the wagon-train, with a company
of Mounted Rifles, Lieutenant Lane having been in command
of Captain Thomas Duncan's company since leaving Fort Mc-
Intosh. Captain Duncan was on leave.

We had a miserable time that day; all our blankets and
shawls in the ambulance were more than damp. When we

came late in the evening to a suitable camp-ground, we sat in
the ambulance waiting until we were exhausted for the rattle
of the wagons; but no such sound came to us, at least not from
our train.

The prospect was gloomy enough; we had nothing to eat
with us, and the soldiers were hungry and wet to the skin.
After watching and hoping against hope that the wagons would
certainly come after a while, a man rode into camp with the information that they were ten miles behind and up to the hubs
in mud! Pleasant prospect for such a night,—pouring rain, and
no provisions! We were in a grove of cotton-wood-trees, and
the men soon started a big fire. It was unnecessary to be cold,
even if wet and hungry. Just at the darkest moment a train of
wagons was heard approaching, and it proved to be one going
down the country empty. The wagon-master was able to supply
the soldiers with rations for a meal, and we glady accepted
some bread, bacon, and coffee from their store, and felt wonderfully cheered after a hot supper. They furnished us with
candles, also.

The prospect for a night's rest was bad; though we were
not actually out in the rain. The ambulance was too small to
lie down in, so we sat up and held the baby on our laps, turn
about. Suddenly she gave one of those hoarse, croupy coughs,
terrifying with the most comfortable surroundings; but it was
distracting, situated as we were, with every wrap more than
moist, and thirty miles from a doctor or house of any kind. By
some good fortune I had a few simple medicines in the ambulance. I lost no time in administering them, and the results
were very gratifying. The night passed and we hailed the
morning with joy.

EIGHT

As SOON AS it was daylight we decided that I with the baby and an escort must go on to Fort Craig, thirty miles away, to see the doctor, leaving husband to follow later with the company. The roads were bad, but we reached Craig early in the afternoon.

Several officers of the regiment were already stationed at the post, among whom were Colonel George B. Crittenden and Colonel Andrew Porter, so I was sure of meeting friends. But it never occurred to us that the fifty-seven consecutive hours of rain that had fallen might have inconvenienced the people at the fort, as well as ourselves. All we wanted was a dry, comfortable room for the baby. What was my dismay when I heard that the dirt roofs of the adobe quarters were leaking all over! Mrs. Porter was quite ill, and the water was pouring into the room where she was in bed under a tent-fly, with an umbrella over her head! Colonel Crittenden's quarters were in the same building, and the rain streamed through the ceiling like a shower-bath; but it was all he had to offer, and, though everything was saturated in the room but the bed, we took it. The rain ceased towards night and large fires were built; but the water still ran in from the roof. I trembled for the baby when I saw where we were to stay, but under the doctor's care she improved at once. Possibly living so long in tents had hardened us, and made us less liable to take cold; we were young, too, and not nervous.

The "lieutenant," with the company, reached Craig late the day I arrived, and the soldiers went into camp just outside the fort. We remained in the quarters several days, taking our meals with Colonel and Mrs. Porter. She recovered before very long from her illness, and found plenty to do to restore order in her drowned-out apartments.

The ground and tents having soon dried in the camp, we decided to leave the still wet walls of the adobe quarters, which we did, and were pleased with the change, being much more comfortable.

Whether it was camping on the Rio Grande or the days we spent in the wet room at Craig, I do not know, but I succumbed, while in camp, to an attack of chills and fever. One night, I remember, husband had to bring the doctor from the fort to see me. During his absence fever came on, and while lying looking up at the tent I saw a centipede five or six inches long, crawling just over my head. I watched it so intently that by the time he and the doctor came the thing had grown as large as an elephant to my fevered imagination, and I could only point to it in terror. It was quickly put out of the way.

When I was able to move we broke camp and began our travels toward Santa Fé, arriving October 9. Santa Fé, at that time, had but a small American population outside of army officers and their families. Mexicans and adobe houses were everywhere, and our surroundings could hardly have been more novel had we been dropped into Spain. We were most delightfully entertained while in the old city by Captain and Mrs. Nicholls. She was a daughter of General De Russy, U.S. Army.

Our station was to be Cantonment Burgwin, four days' march from Santa Fé, over a frightful road, if it could be called "a road." You may go to the foot of any mountain in your neighborhood, start up at any point regardless of stones, holes, or other impediments, and you will have an idea of "the road" to Burgwin. In some places the wagons had to be let down with ropes, and nothing was thought of a drop of two or three feet, from one rock to another. Consequently, we were well shaken up and bruised and battered when the post was reached.

The scenery was magnificent, but we could not enjoy it, owing to the roughness of the road. Did we allow our eyes to wander for a moment to the lofty mountains around us, we were forcibly reminded of the rocks and pitfalls in our path by a jerk or a wrench which dispelled our dreams and brought us rudely back to the immediate surroundings. We stayed at night in Mexican houses, using our own beds, however. Even then, as soon as the light was out we were nearly devoured by bugs, but that was a trifle compared to sleeping in a tent that cold weather.

One night a little puppy got into our room, and made so much noise husband picked him up to put him out of doors. Puppy disliked this treatment, for he seized the thumb of the hand that held him and bit it. For years afterwards the skin peeled off the end of that thumb about the same month, whether in consequence of the bite I do not know, but such was the case.

On the fourth day from Santa Fé we arrived at Burgwin, a very small post, most beautifully situated, being surrounded by high mountains. It was nine miles from Taos, New Mexico. We could stand at our door and talk to our opposite neighbor across the parade-ground without raising our voices. The quarters, though old and out of repair, were comfortable; they were built of rough pine logs; an entry, with rooms on each side.

We added a small Mexican girl to our corps of by no means efficient servants. Our efforts at conversation were necessarily strained, I not speaking Spanish, nor she English; but we soon learned to understand each other with many gestures and a word here and there. It was her business to amuse the baby and wheel the little wagon, which she upset occasionally; consequently the poor child's small turned-up nose seldom had any skin on it while the señorita was nurse, which was not long. Our garrison was a small one,—Major McCrea, with his wife and daughter, Lieutenant Alexander McD. McCook, Lieutenant Alexander McCrea, and ourselves were all the officers and ladies at Burgwin, except a contract doctor, who was drunk half the time, and not of much service. Fortunately it was a healthy place, and he had little to do.

Husband had occasion to go to him for advice one morning, after suffering all night. The doctor looked seriously at him for some time, then said, in solemn tones, "Lane, the best thing you can do is to go home and to bed, until you are sober!" He had been on a spree himself, and imagined it was the other fellow.

We had only been settled in our quarters a few days when we heard of the arrival at Fort Union, New Mexico, of a large number of officers and their families, who had just crossed the Plains from Fort Leavenworth with recruits for the various regiments in the Territory. Among the officers was Captain Washington L. Elliott, who had recently married my sister, who was with him.

Of course the next thing to be done was for husband to go to Fort Union and bring her to Burgwin. She might hear the road was bad, but I knew she could have no conception of what it was like until she tried it, and then it would be too late to turn back.

While I was alone at Burgwin, after husband had left for Fort Union, I had rather a disagreeable experience. In garrison people hardly ever lock their doors, and even when they want to they find the locks broken or keys lost. I could fasten my bedroom door, for which I was thankful. I do not believe there was another lock in the house in order.

One night I was awakened by a knock on my door, which

was repeated. I asked who was there. The answer was a request that "the lady would please open the door" and show a man the way out; that he was drunk, had come in, and had lost himself; that he would do the lady no harm if she would only open the door for him. Needless to say, the lady remained in her fortress, ordering him to leave immediately, or she would call the guard, which she could not have done, as the guard-house was some distance away. After stumbling around in the entry for a while, he left, but returned, later on, though he did not knock again. The man had sense enough to know he had been in an officer's house, but whose he could not tell, so he informed the sentinel. That was the only time I was ever molested by a soldier in all my army experience. I had always found them most polite and respectful. He was a good man, too, but had taken too much whiskey, which was not his habit.

When Captain and Mrs. Elliott arrived it was decided that "the lieutenant" should exchange from Captain Duncan's company to Captain Elliott's, leave Burgwin, and go to Hatch's ranch for the winter, and it was done. We packed up again and left, after a stay of only three weeks at Burgwin.

I would like to tell of some of Lieutenant McCook's pranks at the little cantonment, but he is so very sedate now I would be afraid to do it. He was always happy and good-natured, and was known and liked by Mexicans as well as Americans. Poor Lieutenant McCrea was killed at the battle of Valverde, not far from Fort Craig, New Mexico, in the late war.

On the 4th of November we left, taking the road to Fort Union, which was as bad as the one from Santa Fé; it could not be worse. We were obliged to remain one day at Union, I being quite indisposed, from exposure on the mountains. When we reached the ranch, on the 9th, we found Captain Elliott's company of Mounted Rifles already in quarters, with Lieutenant John Edson in command.

NINE

Wнем we saw the ranch we felt somewhat melancholy at the prospect of spending the winter in such an isolated spot, so far from everywhere.

It stood alone, on slightly rising ground,—a long, low, adobe house, with a high wall all around it, except in front. Mr. Hatch and his wife lived in one part of the building, and, with the exception of our own little party, were the only white people to be seen.

We had just room enough to be comfortable; but it was well we were one family, for we were very close together, and to have had strangers in the house would have been unbearable. There was no doctor nearer than seventy-five or eighty miles, so we tried to keep well. A Mexican man and his wife went about sometimes to officiate in particular cases. I had the luck to be present on one occasion. I think their performances would have made the scientific physicians of the present day open their eyes. Lieutenant Edson went on leave shortly after our arrival, and when we met again he had married lovely Fannie Clark.

We passed a very quiet, though pleasant, winter; but we were by no means sorry when the company was ordered to Fort Union in the spring. The post seemed very gay to us, with the band and so many people. We had seen no one but each other for such a long time, we were quite bewildered with all the stir and bustle about us. The quarters being large enough to accommodate us all, we remained with Captain and Mrs. Elliott.

In July I decided to take a leave and go East with the baby. Colonel Benjamin Roberts and family, with some discharged soldiers as escort, were taking advantage of an empty train of Mexican wagons, leaving New Mexico for Kansas City, to bring back a load of goods for all parts of the Territory. I joined the party. We were to have a great big ten-mule wagon in which we were to travel and sleep. Husband had a spring-bottom made for the floor, on which a mattress was laid, and we lived in the wagon about four weeks. Colonel Roberts had two wagons for his family. We messed with them, some of the discharged soldiers cooking for us.

Husband travelled with us for a few days, to see that we were entirely comfortable, and then returned to Fort Union.

The wagon-train was in charge of a Mexican wagon-master, and he alone decided where we were to camp and when to travel. It seemed to make no difference to him where he halted, nor whether wood and water were convenient or not. Sometimes, late in the afternoon, the wagons were driven off the road, corralled, and the mules sent to graze. We felt confident then we would stay there until morning. Our supper would be cooked and eaten with good, healthy appetites, though it usually consisted only of hot biscuit, fried bacon, coffee, and buffalo meat or other game, killed by the teamsters.

At a very early hour we were quite ready for bed, and we would crawl into our wagons, have the covers well secured, and hope for a quiet night. Often just as I had fallen into a good sleep I was roused by a stir in the camp, the distant sound of the mules galloping towards the wagons, and the clatter of the bell on the neck of the herd-leader, a forlorn old gray mule with both ears cut off close to his head. When it rained the bell kept up a constant tinkle as the water fell into the holes which naturally should have been covered, and annoyed the poor creature very much, so that he wagged his head continually. I believe he had been captured from the Indians, who probably cut off his ears and ate them, to show how they loved him. The more agony the wretched beast suffered, the more his tormentors enjoyed it, only sorry he was not human.

The noise made by the mules and the teamsters put an end to sleep. How they ever knew one mule from another in the darkness was a mystery to me; but they seemed to, and in a shorter time than it takes to write it, each driver had his team harnessed, hitched to the wagon, and we were off for an all-night ride. Possibly by eight or nine o'clock next morning we would halt long enough to rest the mules and get breakfast, then start again.

I never slept when we travelled at night; the wagon was rough, notwithstanding the spring bottom. As a rule the road was fine; but I do not suppose the tired and sleepy driver was very careful to keep in it, so that we had many unnecessary jolts.

One night we were travelling slowly, when it began to rain; I was wide awake, listening to the patter of the drops on the wagon-sheet. I felt more than usually lonely and helpless, for, by some mistake, there was a wagon between mine and the one occupied by Colonel Roberts's family; so that, if I needed assistance, I could not be heard by them, call as loud as I might. Suddenly I was conscious that some one was untying the cover, which was always fastened down securely after I got into the wagon at night. Then by the dim light I could make out the figure of a man creeping in, and he sat down just at my feet. I did not make a sound, but quietly reached out my hand to a basket by my mattress, and took out a big butcher-knife, which I always kept there,—not for defensive purposes, however. The man sat perfectly quiet; but I thought he might murder us for the little we had, take a mule from the team, and escape. I certainly would have used my knife had he molested me, and I never took my eyes off him all night. When day dawned the man retired as noiselessly as he came, and proved to be the Mexican who drove my wagon. I lost no time in telling Colonel Roberts of my night's alarm, and another teamster was sent to take the place of my too friendly driver, who told the wagonmaster he only wanted to get out of the rain. The mules had taken care of themselves all night, following the wagon ahead of them.

In those days the whole country was covered with immense herds of buffalo; there were thousands and thousands of them; yes, a million. They never molested the trains crossing the Plains, though sometimes a great drove of them came thundering down to the road, and the wagons were obliged to halt until they passed. There was no difficulty in killing one when fresh meat was needed; but the wary hunter seldom wandered far away, as there were plenty of Indians abroad as well as buffalo. A man strayed off one day, and we knew nothing of him until night, when he came into camp, naked. Indians had caught him while hunting, taken all his clothes, even his shoes, and then turned him adrift. He kept at a respectful distance from the wagons until darkness covered him,—the only mantle he had,—and then came into camp. He did not care much for hunting during the rest of his travels.

We saw a man shoot a buffalo one day, and as the great beast fell when the bullet struck him, we all thought he was dead, and so did the hunter, until he ran up close to him to cut his throat, when the creature rose up and made a spring, which scared the man dreadfully, being entirely unexpected. He ran for dear life, with the wounded buffalo in hot pursuit. Fortunately there was a saddled horse not far off, which the bold hunter succeeded in mounting, and was soon far away. Like a predecessor, "he never looked behind him." The hunts were very exciting, and usually took place quite near the wagons, so that we could see all that went on. We needed something to vary the wearisome march. One variation I did not like at all, and that was the vicinity of so many Indians, who often rode close beside our wagon staring in at the baby, who with her light curly hair and blue eyes seemed to interest them amazingly. I tried to keep her out of sight, but she never was one easy to suppress, and kept me in an agony by evidently enjoying the admiration she excited. They never interfered with us, however, our party being too large for them to feel certain of victory if they made the fight. I was truly rejoiced when we got away from their haunts and hunting-grounds. They roamed the plains in the summer season, killing the buffalo, curing meat, and dressing the hides for their winter supplies.

I used to watch the Mexican teamsters drying buffalo meat, or "jerking" it, with much interest. It was cut into thin, narrow strips, and hung up in the sun on ropes stretched across the camp from wagon to wagon. When we were ready to leave the meat was taken down, packed in "gunny-sacks," and tramped and stamped upon to make it less bulky. Then it was stowed away in the wagons and taken out and sunned at every camp. No salt is used in jerking the meat, and to me it is horrible; but I suppose if brought to the verge of starvation I might be able to relish it—hardly otherwise.

We travelled rapidly from Fort Union to Kansas City, making the distance of six hundred miles in twenty-four days. We stopped at the principal hotel in the town, being driven to it in our ten-mule wagons. What a sensation we would make now, by arriving in that style! Then no one gave us a second look. Such sights were of daily occurrence. Before railroads were built trains of wagons were always to be seen going to and coming from the Territories.

TEN

THE JOURNEY FROM Kansas City to St. Louis, and from there to Carlisle, Pa., took a good deal of time. We travelled from St. Louis alone, but many a kind hand was stretched out to help us when we needed assistance.

How delightful it was to be at home once more! Of course the first grandchild was an important person, and came in for a large share of attention and admiration, which she received with all the coolness and matter-of-course air of one who had seen much of the world and was accustomed to it. I had been gone nearly three years, and many changes had taken place in that time,—marriages, births, and deaths among my relatives.

I had been so long deprived of everything but the bare necessaries of life, it seemed to me my friends lived luxuriously, and I enjoyed my visit to the fullest extent.

The greatest drawback to my happiness, while at home, was the time required for letters to come from and go to New Mexico,—a whole month between mails, which were carried on a stage, running between Independence, Missouri, and Santa Fé, New Mexico. The mail stations on the plains were few and far apart, where there were only enough hardy, determined men to look after the mules required for the stage. These stations were almost fortresses on a small scale, built of stone, with a high wall around them to protect the stock from Indians. The stage-drivers were experienced frontiersmen, who knew well the risks they ran, and those who travelled with them have told me there was no time lost between stations, going at a full gallop most of the way. Often wild and unbroken animals were harnessed to the stage, and at the first crack of the whip they were off with a bound, and kept at a run or gallop, never slowing up until the house was in sight.

I remained at home almost a year. In the mean time, Captain Elliott's company had been moved to Fort Stanton, New Mexico, and husband had gone with it. At the end of my leave, as several officers and their families were going to Fort Leavenworth from Carlisle Barracks, we joined them. From Fort Leavenworth we were to cross the Plains with a large number of officers and recruits for the regiments in New Mexico, and were to travel with Colonel Charles Ruff and family, who were to be of the party, camping near and messing with them. We had our own ambulance and tent, and were quite independent. I had taken a young black child from home as a playmate for our little girl, and she was in a constant state of excitement at the novelty of her situation, causing much amusement by her comments on matters in general.

Colonel Ruff remained at Leavenworth a day after the command left; but as Lieutenant Edson and wife were among those starting out, we went with them. At the first camp there was always a good deal of confusion, as things were put into the wagons helter-skelter, and some time was required to find tents, pins, ropes, axes, etc., and the recruits were rather new at the business of pitching tents. All was ready at last, beds were made, and everything comfortable for the night, when one of those awful Kansas storms burst upon us almost without warning. The wind (now called a cyclone) was terrific, and the lightning and thunder a fit accompaniment to such a gale. Many of the tents, not being pitched to withstand as fierce a battle, went down all over over the camp. Ours rocked and shook, and the roar of the thunder and the rain beating on the canvas was deafening.

Lieutenant Edson, seeing my tent was not secure, came, in the midst of the downpour, and took us to his, which was better pitched, and we were hardly out of ours before it collapsed. With my party, added to Mrs. Edson and servant, theirs was full, and Lieutenant Edson went elsewhere for shelter. The storm raged on; by degrees the tent-cords loosened, the walls were blown in and out with the wind, and we expected every moment to see it share the fate of many others, but the few pins left and the guy-ropes held it up. The water rushed in a torrent through the tent, and the only way to keep out of it was to sit on the bed, which we did until morning. An old sow, with her large family, tried to take shelter under the canvas wall also, and it was extremely difficult to keep her out: she did not like the warring elements for her babies any more than we did.

The camp was a dismal sight next day,—everything and everybody were soaking wet and felt as dreary as they looked. Bedding and clothing were spread in every available spot to dry, and the tents re-pitched, as we could not well move in such a plight to another camp. All had a tale to tell of the awful night. One tent blew down in which was a child asleep on a cot. The wind gathered them up, but the child was seen, fortunately, and dragged off by some one as the bed went sailing over a fence. The flagstaff at Fort Leavenworth, seven miles away, was struck by lightning the same night.

We took up our line of march next day, although our belongings were still in a wet and forlorn condition. The storms followed us, and I never beheld such lightning nor heard such thunder. When I saw one coming we went into the tent and had it well pinned down and the opening closed securely. Through all its fury I had to look as if I liked it, not daring to show fear before the children, and I am sure I must have been fairly green with fright sometimes. But we played, told stories, and sang songs, the howling wind and crashing thunder joining in the chorus, and by controlling myself before the children I lost much of my own terror. But I must say I was delighted to get out of the storm region.

We passed through several villages of half-civilized Indians in Kansas, and the sight of them filled Kit, the black child, with horror. A man came and stood by the tent one day, watching her attentively; he seemed to be trying to work out an idea. At last his curiosity got the better of him and I found out what the trouble was. He said to me, looking at Kit, "Dat you pappoose?" Before I could answer, she spoke, from her safe place behind the bed, "No, sir; I am Mr. Hawkins's girl, of Carlisle," which information was received with a grunt; he could not understand a white squaw having a black pappoose, and wanted to be certain about it.

The rivers in Kansas were deep, and hard to ford. No one knew just where the proper crossings were to be found, and much time was lost looking for them. There did not seem to be any one with the command whose business it was to find out about such matters, and we had to get information from any one whom we happened to meet on the road. Being impatient to go on, I may have imagined there was mismanagement. However, this much I know, that frequently, when hunting a ford, the command was directed to a certain point; when it was reached there was not a place where we could cross, and we had to retrace our steps, going possibly just as far the other way, to find the stream over the tops of the wagons. Delay seemed to be the order of the day. One morning, after everything was ready for the usual early start, breakfast over, tents down, and wagons loaded, the news was brought in that every mule belonging to the wagon-train had gone, and not a man knew how nor when they left. Of course some one was to blame for gross negligence; but that did not help matters in the least.

Nothing could be done but unpack the wagons, re-pitch tents, and remain on Cow Creek until something was found to haul us away. Parties were sent to look for the mules, but to this day nothing has been heard of them,—a remarkable truth.

For a week we remained in camp waiting for transportation, when at the end of that time some one saw, as did "Sister Anne" in the story of Blue Beard, a little cloud of dust in the west. It proved to be from an empty ox-train which was coming to the States, and it meant relief for us. The oxen were put to our wagons, their heads turned towards New Mexico, and we were again on the road.

Fortunately, none of the ambulance mules had departed when those belonging to the train left it so mysteriously.

As we could travel only short distances with the oxen every day, the time seemed long and exceedingly tedious. Two months passed before we reached Fort Union, a journey of six hundred miles. There I heard of a campaign against the Navajo Indians, and that husband had gone with Captain Elliott and company from Fort Stanton, to join other troops sent out to Fort Defiance, in the Navajo country. This was indeed bad news for me, as I had expected to find him waiting for us at Fort Union, instead of which he had gone to fight Indians, and might be away all winter. There was nothing for me to do but to make my way to my sister, Mrs. Elliott, at Fort Stanton, which was a great way off, and not an easy place to reach. Besides, I could not always get an escort from post to post, so that I made slow progress.

We remained some days at Fort Union with Captain and Mrs. Shoemaker, who were always glad of an opportunity to take the weary traveller under their most hospitable roof and care for him.

From Fort Union we went to Santa Fé, in October, rested a few days, and then left for Albuquerque, where we arrived after three days' travel, and were the guests of Colonel and Mrs. Ruff, who had just gone to housekeeping in the old Mexican town, after having recently crossed the Plains. Colonel Ruff and Major Rucker, with their families, occupied a large adobe building; each had a part of it, entirely independent of the other. At that time Irene Rucker was a little child playing about in her blue check aprons, little dreaming she was destined to be the wife of the gallant General Sheridan.

On THE FIRST of November Colonel I. V. D. Reeve left Albuquerque for Fort Stanton, and we gladly accepted his escort. We had been travelling since the beginning of July, and I was tired and wanted to settle down. Six days were required to make the distance between the two points, with a house to stay in two or three nights out of the five or six. The weather was cold, and I much preferred to stay in a house where there was fire than in a tent with none.

One night, when in camp, it rained hard, then snowed. The tents froze stiff, and it was with difficulty they could be made small enough to be packed in the wagon next morning. We had a bitter cold ride all that day, and when we camped, at night, it was in the frozen tents on top of ice and snow, which had to be cut away to make a place for the mattress. Minnie and Kit did not seem at all disturbed at going to bed on top of the snow. We slept in all of our clothes, rolling our heads in shawls; but it was so cold and uncomfortable we were glad there was but one night of it.

It was with grateful hearts we reached the cosey quarters at Fort Stanton at last, and were soon entirely at home at my sister's house, where we remained until the husbands returned from the Navajo war, when we occupied our own quarters.

Fort Stanton was a beautiful post, with the best quarters in the army at that time, but it was like being buried alive to stay there. Nothing ever passed that way, and it was seldom a stranger came among us. There was but one mail a month, and on the day it was expected we dropped all work and fixed our eyes on a certain hill, round which the man with the mail, carried on a mule, was bound to appear, after a while, if the Indians had not caught him. Whoever first spied him spread the news that the mail was coming. Then all was excitement until the post-office was opened and each had his own letters and papers in his hands. Although the papers were old, we enjoyed their contents as much as we do our "daily" of to-day.

An officer's wife told me she gave her husband only one paper at a time, and laid it by his plate, on the breakfast-table, every morning, as long as they lasted, hoping he would try to imagine he was reading "news." We wanted ours all at once, even if we did have to wait a month for a fresh supply.

We were fortunate in having a pleasant garrison at Fort Stanton, and our relations with the officers and their wives were most sociable and friendly. There were no formal visits then, nor did we have occasion to dress up to call on our neighbors. To show you of how little use a bonnet was to any of us, sweet little Mrs. Lawrence Baker had forgotten hers entirely, until, one day, when looking over her possessions, she found it occupied by a hen, setting on a number of eggs. The style of bonnet at that time made a very comfortable nest, quite different from those of to-day.

My sister had a piano, which was an unbounded source of pleasure to us. With Colonel Reeve's assistance we made quite good music; at least our friends, who, possibly, were not too critical, said so. Kind, good Colonel Reeve, always anxious and ready to be of service when we needed it. (He died January, 1891, in New York.)

The Mescalero Apaches were in camp that winter near the post, and came and went as they pleased, walking into our houses and sitting on our porches without the least hesitation. I found a young fellow in front of our quarters with a child's

colored picture-book in his hands, chuckling and muttering
with great delight. Coming closer, I saw he was holding it upside down, and turned it for him. He was much pleased and
surprised when he was able to understand the pictures, and
laughed and talked quietly to himself. I do not suppose he had
ever seen a book before.

I never could become accustomed to the Indians staring at
me through the window when I was sewing or reading. Often
while sitting beside it a shadow would come between me and
the light, and on looking up I would find two or three hideous
creatures, with noses painted every color flattened against the
glass. I would move away at once, out of range of their wondering eyes. I could not endure to be watched so curiously. Sometimes a slight noise made me turn round, and there would be
one or two Indians standing in my room. I did not use much
ceremony in putting them out and locking the door behind
them. They delighted in going to the hospital to get a dose of
medicine from the doctor; and no matter what kind of stuff he
mixed them, they took it with apparent enjoyment. I do not
know that a dose of medicine, taken when there was no necessity for it, was worse than (or as bad as) eating a mule with a
sore back, that had died in the corral. They cut him in pieces,
carried the meat to their camp, and ate it all up, everything but
bones and hoofs. A dead mule is not to be despised when one is
starving.

My sister and I found an Indian woman sitting on the
ground by our house, one cold winter's day, and leaning
against her was a board, on which was strapped a new-born
baby, which we learned afterwards was about two hours old!
The woman intimated she was hungry and we gave her food,
when she picked up her baby and walked three miles to camp.
Before we saw her, she and her baby had taken a swim in the
little river that flowed close by; the water was frozen hard, and

she broke the ice to make a place large enough for her purpose. I do not know whether all new-born Apache babies were treated to an ice-cold bath; it must have been disagreeable.

While at Stanton we saw the yearly distribution of presents to the Apaches. The men and women sat or lay on the ground in a circle, inside of which stood some of the officers and ladies of the post, to witness this rather novel sight, to many of us at least. I had only been there a little while until I wished myself anywhere else. As each article was handed round, the Indians became more and more excited; and when the butcher-knives were brought out, deep guttural sounds from the men and screams of delight from the women were heard on all sides. I felt as if we were going to be scalped, and I am sure the recipients of these treasures would not have been at all averse to trying them, bright, new, and sharp, on us, if it could have been done with safety to themselves. I never wanted to see another distribution of presents to Indians, nor to be in the vicinity when hatchets and knives were passed around.

In May orders were received for Captain Elliott's company to take station at Fort Bliss, Texas, and we were charmed at the prospect of going where we would see more people and have a good market. There was never anything to buy at Fort Stanton but an occasional piece of venison, or a wild turkey, from a Mexican or Indian. The game was very good of its kind, but we wanted a wider range, which we were sure to have at Fort Bliss.

By the 19th of May we were packed and ready to leave Stanton. Our only regret was parting with our friends. We travelled over some beautiful country, camping every night. The weather was good, though extremely hot in the middle of the day. We passed several mounds of pure white, silver sand, on the road, which in the distance looked like snow; their pres-

ence in such a place was curious, and has never been explained
to me.

May 25 found us at the most delightful station we ever had,
—Fort Bliss,—the old and first Fort Bliss, far more pleasant
than those of the same name which have succeeded it, though
the present post is more pretentious in every way, having two
railroads running across the parade-ground.

Our quarters of three rooms were of adobe, with thatched
roof and dirt floors; it sounds worse than it was, for the floor
was as hard as stone, almost; and with canvas nailed down first,
and a carpet over that, we were well fixed. Some of the other
quarters were more roomy and pleasant than ours; but we did
not require anything better, and, as we still messed with Captain and Mrs. Elliott, they answered very well.

The garrison at Fort Bliss was very small, but there were
some very pleasant people (citizens) living at and not very far
from the post. There was a good deal of social visiting among
us all, and an occasional formal entertainment, to which everybody was invited.

Colonel Magoffin, the sutler, had a large house, and several
pretty, well-educated daughters. Mrs. Magoffin was a Spanish
woman, from whom the daughters inherited much grace and
beauty. Of course they were great belles, and their home was
very attractive.

At that time Fort Bliss was built on three sides of a square;
a road in front of the quarters separated them from the parade-
ground, which was enclosed by an adobe wall. There were
some tall cottonwood-trees on the parade, which was covered
by a luxuriant growth of alfalfa, or Mexican clover. Perhaps
there was a flag-staff, too, but I forget.

Almost at our doors flowed the red, muddy waters of the
Rio Grande, which were ever encroaching on the banks and
endangering those quarters that were near.

Three miles away was the little town of Franklin,—now El Paso,—where we made frequent visits to buy our marketing and lay in supplies of delicious fresh fruits, furnished by the Mexicans, who interested us very much. Besides the market were several stores, where everything imaginable was sold, not always just what we wanted, however; but we frequently had to take what we could get. Once, when passing through that region, my shoes gave out entirely, and I was obliged to have some at once. The only thing I could find that fitted me at all was a pair of light blue kid slippers, not exactly suitable for travelling and camping, but all that were to be had.

TWELVE

By CROSSING THE Rio Grande we were in a foreign
country,—Mexico,—where everything was so quaint and
strange we could scarcely believe only a narrow river separated
us from our homes.

We went over once to visit the old cathedral, where the
most striking things we saw were some ghastly wax figures,
large as life, and very precious in the sight of the numerous
worshippers. On a table in the centre of the church was laid
what we supposed was another wax image; but on closer inspection we found it was a poor little dead baby, gayly dressed,
and awaiting burial. No one seemed to be watching, and the
tiny thing looked lonely in the big church. I was told it was
customary, both in Old and New Mexico, to dress up a dead
child in bright clothes, crown the head with flowers, and carry
it around the town, with a band of music playing the liveliest
airs.

Even those who had died of small-pox were exhibited, and,
of course, the disease was spread in this way, very few of the
natives being vaccinated. There was always more or less small-
pox in Mexican towns, but, as it seldom attacked Americans,
we had little fear of it, though, when going to a station close to
a Mexican settlement, we took the precaution to be vaccinated.

Once husband was in a town where a fiesta (or festival)
was held, and he became interested in a game going on in the
street, taking no notice of his surroundings, until, just at his
feet, a Mexican woman, sitting on the ground, unrolled a bun-

dle on her lap, which proved to be a baby covered with small-pox. He did not wait to see the end of the game.

In the same town lived an American merchant, with whom we dealt occasionally. One day he asked me to go into his house to see his wife, who was a Spanish woman, and I went, though I only knew enough of her language to ask her how she was, nor could she speak English. So we sat smiling and bowing at each other, looking very silly, no doubt, when I remembered there was a baby, and I managed to ask, in Spanish, how it was. Her face changed at once, and she tried her best to make me understand it was not well, pointing her finger to her forehead and cheeks in such a significant way I was certain the child had small-pox. I did not feel very comfortable, but thought I would sit a little longer.

In a few moments the lady opened a door and called the nurse, who came in with the baby in her arms. One glance, and I fled. Its little yellow face was spotted all over with what I took to be small-pox; but I did not stop to ask any questions, running through the store and into the street to our carriage before I drew breath. I have no doubt my rapid flight amazed the polite little Spanish woman, and that she thought the Señora Americano had gone suddenly crazy. That was coming a little too close to such a loathsome disease for comfort, and after that experience I made no visits unless I knew more about the people on whom I was calling.

We had been but a short time at Fort Bliss when Captain Elliott's servants, a man, his wife, and daughter, all slaves, were induced against their own inclinations to secure their freedom by crossing the Rio Grande into Mexico. Their departure upset our domestic arrangements very materially, as all were good, capable servants, apparently happy and satisfied with their treatment. They found out the mistake in leaving, too late. They returned of their own accord, wretched and penitent, but the once pleasant and comfortable home was theirs no longer. Captain Elliott had always told them if they left him he would never have them again, and he kept his word, sorry as we all were to part with them, and, heart-broken as they were, he sold them to a rich man near Fort Bliss. They realized too late what they had lost.

Our second daughter was born at Fort Bliss early in the fall, and as she had more comfortable surroundings and better care than her sister, she took a more cheerful view of life, and behaved quite well. A little, old Irish camp-woman took care of her. She had much true Irish wit, and her small, withered face was full of fun. A thick, close-fitting white muslin cap with a deep ruffle hanging from it added to her comical expression.

Kit, the little black child, was extremely ill that summer, and we thought she would die; but she lived to return to the bosom of her family, marry, and kill herself at last by falling down stairs.

In the fall, husband applied for a year's leave of absence. He had been on the frontier for five years, and thought he would like a change. The leave was granted, and we made preparations to go East about the middle of October. Mrs. Elliott and baby, her two step-children, and Mexican nurse were to go with us, leaving Captain Elliott at Fort Bliss.

We disliked giving up our pleasant station, where we had been so comfortable and happy. The quarters were tolerably good, and there were fewer insects and snakes than at some other places where we had lived. I only remember seeing one snake, and that was on the bedroom floor. When I awoke one morning I saw what I took to be a curiously striped piece of ribbon. My suspicions were aroused, however, and we soon found out what it was and killed it. We supposed it fell from the thatched roof to the floor. There was no ceiling in the rooms, so that the rafters and thatching were distinctly visible, and there was nothing to prevent a snake dropping in on us whenever he felt inclined.

We left Fort Bliss for San Antonio on the 13th of October with an escort and enough men to pitch our tents. Mrs. Elliott and her family had an ambulance for themselves, while we used one belonging to an army officer who wanted it sent to San Antonio, so we were mutually accommodated.

We had four mules in our team which husband was to drive the whole six hundreds miles, and he did it in a very creditable manner. Many an anxious day and night we spent on that journey. The Indians were ever on the lookout for small parties, and eternal vigilance was required to keep them at bay, and "the lieutenant" was always on the alert.

Our camps were kept as dark as possible at night, no fires nor candles were allowed, but such precautions were often useless, for, just when everything should have been quiet, one or other baby was sure to set up such a roar "as might have been heard ten miles or more."

I quake now, when I think what risks we ran travelling with small escorts. Nothing but constant watchfulness on the part of Lieutenant Lane and his few men kept us from being attacked. Indians were more afraid of soldiers then, and had more respect for them than now, and travellers with a military escort, when careful, were not often molested, unless the Indians far outnumbered them and were sure of the result. A bow with poisoned arrows was the Indians' principal weapon, and it was seldom that a good gun was found among them; hence their respect for a well-armed soldier.

Woe to the hapless party that fell into the devilish hands of a band of Indians! Men were generally put to death by slow torture, but they were allowed to live long enough to witness the atrocities practised on their wives and children, such things as only fiends could devise. Babies had their brains dashed out before the eyes of father and mother, powerless to help them. Lucky would the latter have been, had they treated her in the same way; but what she was forced to endure would have wrung tears from anything but an Indian. Do you wonder at our dread of them?

The country between Fort Bliss and Fort Davis was particularly adapted to Indian warfare. Numerous trains of wagons and bands of emigrants had been attacked and destroyed at some of the water-holes on that road. Van Horn's Well, Eagle Spring, and Dead Man's Hole were favorite watering-places and camp-grounds. Dreary, desolate spots they were, as many an army officer and soldier, and women not a few, can testify.

Our little camp of four or five tents, two ambulances, and possibly three wagons, looked lonesome enough, with but a handful of men and two or three women and some little children; not another living thing to be seen, except the mules.

It was a pleasure to us when we reached an army post where we were safe, and for that day, at least, could relax our vigilance. We met with kind friends everywhere, who supplied us with many comforts which could not be purchased.

We stayed over at Fort Davis, where wagons, etc., were repaired and everything put to rights that required attention. The people whom we met in 1856, when the Rifle Regiment passed there, *en route* to New Mexico, were all gone; but those who replaced them were equally kind, and anxious to help us in any way.

We had a funny time at Camp (now Fort) Stockton, our next halting-place; at least it is funny now to remember. As there were some quarters vacant, we went into them, while we remained, as we had more room than in the tents to examine our camping "outfit," mend clothes, etc.

The first thing we did was to make inquiries for a laundress, as we had been without one for some time. Unfortunately for us, the day to "lie over" was Sunday, and not a camp-woman at the post would do anything for us, which might speak well for their piety; but I am inclined to think they had something more entertaining on hand for the day, and, having worked hard all week, did not care to put themselves out to accommodate us. Here was an unlooked-for dilemma; we were obliged to leave next day, and must find a laundress somewhere.

After a consultation it became very evident that if there was to be any washing done that Sunday morning, the ladies must do it themselves; and we went to work, borrowed tubs and boards, rolled up our sleeves in true laundress style, and did our best.

The results were far from satisfactory; though we used all our energy and strength, the articles looked rather worse than before they had passed through our unskillful hands. We were not much elated at our first attempt at washing clothes, and did not try to iron them.

THIRTEEN

W E LEFT CAMP STOCKTON next day with a large train of empty wagons, returning to San Antonio, and Lieutenant Lane took control of it, to the evident disgust of the wagonmaster, who hoped to have matters all his own way, halting and leaving camp as suited his own convenience. He was a small, lame man, with a villainous countenance, who never obeyed an order without a protest. His conduct was almost mutinous, and I feared trouble from him and his teamsters, as he had influence with them, and turned them against "the lieutenant." All this, added to my anxiety about Indians, made the journey anything but pleasant.

The man gave in at last, knowing he must obey or fight; but he was always sullen and disagreeable.

Again I saw Camp Lancaster, the worst of all the posts in Texas. The road to it led over a hill, which was even worse than those we crossed going to Burgwin, and exceeds my descriptive powers. I had laughed when told of this dreadful hill, and my friend said she knew I would not ride down it; I replied I never got out of the ambulance, no matter how bad the road might be. When I came to the top of it and saw what was before me, I pulled open the door of the ambulance, and was on the ground in a second and walked to the bottom of the hill. How ambulances and wagons ever went up and down such a place without being dashed to pieces I cannot imagine, but then nothing ever seemed to happen to army wagons.

We found Fort Clark much improved since we had lived

there, in the little shanty in the chaparral. General French was in command, and entertained us most kindly.

Five or six days later we reached San Antonio, and were thankful the most dangerous part of the road was passed.

The quartermaster at once discharged the insubordinate wagon-master when the case was laid before him, whereupon the man sent word to Lieutenant Lane he was going to kill him, but he changed his mind.

As the yellow fever was epidemic in some of the towns through which we must pass to reach the coast, we were obliged to delay our departure for the North, and decided to visit Austin until the weather became cold enough for frost or until the fever abated. An addition of ten people, large and small, made a material change in the household of Dr. and Mrs. Lane; but, with true Southern hospitality, they would not hear of our going anywhere else to stay.

By the 4th of December it was thought safe for us to begin our travels towards the coast through the country where the fever had recently raged.

When we left Austin, in the stage, the day was very hot. There had been enough frost before that time, however, to put an end to the epidemic for that season. As night drew on, an unmistakable puff of cool wind announced the coming of a norther, and by the time the town was reached where we were to change horses we were suffering with the cold. We were tired out from our day's ride, and still had the prospect of an all-night journey before us. It took some time to get the weary, sleepy children out of the stage and into the house, where the warmth of a bright wood-fire comforted us all wonderfully. By this time it was blowing and raining hard, the rain freezing as it fell. The stage only stopped at this place long enough to change horses usually, but the ice-cold norther paralyzed the negro hostlers, and it was hours before all were ready to leave.

Instead of the regular coach, a "mud-wagon" had been substituted, on account of the dangerous condition of the roads, which were frozen and very slippery.

What a fearful night we passed! There were ten in our party, including the baby, a very important member of it, as she ran equal chances of freezing or smothering. How we all managed to pack in the wagon, with several other passengers, I do not know. I remember my shawl had slipped off my shoulders, and I was utterly powerless and unable to get it around me again, and no one could assist me unless I stood up. I managed to stagger to my feet, holding the baby in my arms. Then I found I could neither stand nor get back to my seat. I cried out for help, that the baby would freeze to death, and some one, finally, was able to plant me in the half-dozen inches of seat again. I made no more attempts to rise. The men passengers spent most of the night walking; the roads were in such a state the horses could not pull the heavy load. Mr. Lane walked, too, rolled in a Navajo blanket to protect himself from the sleet; by morning it was frozen stiff on him. The driver had frequently to ask for help from the men, and when we reached the stopping-place, next morning, the poor fellows were almost exhausted, and we were so cramped and tired we were hardly able to walk.

The house seemed delightfully comfortable after our cold night-ride, and we were not much distressed when told we would not be able to leave the town for several days. There was a rope-ferry over the river, and as soon as the norther came all hands struck work and could not be induced to do anything. No use to grumble; there the passengers must wait until the norther blew itself out.

The house was small and pretty well filled, when we arrived, with storm-stayed people from various points. There was but one room left for all of us, and beds were put on the floor. There was plenty to eat, and we were satisfied, or, at least, we accepted the situation cheerfully.

We were glad, however, when it was announced the stage would leave "that day." Being the earliest arrivals from Austin, we were entitled to seats in the first coach that left. We could have sold our privilege for a high price, but we were anxious to get on, and paid no attention to hints thrown out by those quite as desirous of leaving as we were.

We found the men at the ferry sufficiently thawed to get us across the river safely, and we said goodby gladly to Chappell Hill, Texas, though it had been a haven of rest to us after that ride in the bitter cold storm.

Several of the small towns through which we passed were almost depopulated by yellow fever; in some of them there were scarcely enough people left to bury the dead. At Houston we were obliged to stay half a day at the hotel, which had just been reopened, after having been closed some time on account of the fever. This seemed to bring us rather too close to it, but there was no danger of taking the disease after the frost.

We had a ride on the only railroad at that time in Texas; the best thing I can say of it was, it was very short. From the cars we went aboard a steamboat, which passed through bayous so narrow she frequently scraped the banks and was shoved off with long poles. No outlet was visible, so numerous were the twists and turns. But the boat kept on her winding way until she entered a broad sheet of water, and soon after Galveston was reached. We were obliged to remain there a day or two, waiting for a steamer to cross the Gulf of Mexico for New Orleans. We did not particularly crave the three days' voyage, but as no other route was then open to us, we were soon on board the big ship and steaming out of the Galveston harbor. As has always been my experience in travelling, the domestics were useless. Kit and Marie, the Mexican nurse, were at once over come and unable to do anything. None of us suffered at all from sea-sickness, nor did the children, although the passage was not particularly smooth. I remember the ship gave a lurch one day while husband was dressing in the state-room, and his head went through a looking-glass which hung over the wash-stand. We were not superstitious, and, as no cuts or bruises resulted, we did not give it another thought. Not all of our fellow-passengers fared as well as we did, however, regarding sea-sickness. One was a bright boy, about twelve years old, whom I noticed when we left Galveston and not again until we were going off the ship. I asked if he had been sea-sick. He said, "Yes, very; too ill to eat anything, although he had paid for his passage and *meals* before leaving Galveston." He spoke in an injured tone and felt badly treated.

From New Orleans to Carlisle it was a series of staging and railroading; tedious delays were frequent. It did not seem of the least consequence whether trains were run on time or not. There were no Pullman cars then, and we had to do the best we could when travelling at night. Sometimes changes had to be made after we had gone to sleep, and great confusion was the result, to collect the children, bundles, etc. If we had not been so interested we would have found it amusing to watch the Mexican girl getting out of the cars. She never had seen one before, and was not used to going up- and down-stairs in the adobe shanties at home. She would stand on the platform of the car, put one foot on the step and bring the other down beside it, standing still for a second or two, trying to hold her dress closely around her ankles; then she would go through the same thing until she reached the ground, and we were ready to shake her for her delay.

She almost had a convulsion the first time she heard a steam-engine whistle.

In Mississippi we had another tedious stage-ride of a day

and part of the night. The coach was packed full, of course, and the poor children had to sit on any lap that would accommodate them. The mud was two feet deep, and the men passengers had to assist in digging the stage out of the mire with fence-rails several times during the day. It was midnight when we reached the railroad again. There was not a house anywhere about, in which we could get a room to rest, and we were in despair. After a while, some men connected with the railroad took compassion on the poor tired children, and let us go into a baggage-car, filled with mail-bags, over which we spread some shawls, lay down, and slept soundly until the cars were ready to leave next morning.

When we arrived at Washington a question arose about allowing Kit to be taken from a slave State into a free one without certain papers, although she was born free. We were delayed some time while the matter was discussed, and at last "the lieutenant's" patience became exhausted, and he told the man they could keep her, which made the child almost white from fright. Finally, consent was given for her to leave, the authorities being satisfied she was not a slave.

FOURTEEN

WE FINISHED OUR travels just before Christmas. What a comfort it was to find a good nurse ready for the baby, and be able to rest after having been on the road since the middle of October, two months.

Notwithstanding a whole year's leave had been granted when the application was made, husband was ordered back to New Mexico the next summer. He went on to New York and laid his case before "the powers," all to no purpose. Lorenzo Thomas was then adjutant-general to General Winfield Scott, and not noted for his suave manner nor kindly feeling towards young officers. The interview between the two gentlemen was stormy, which, perhaps, did "the lieutenant's" cause more harm than good; but he had the satisfaction of expressing his opinion on his own case as well as some others.

My sister, Mrs. Elliott, never returned to the frontier. She went to housekeeping in Carlisle, where Captain Elliott joined her some time afterwards.

When we found we must go back to New Mexico, we made hasty preparations, and were most fortunate in securing two excellent colored women to take with us.

The nurse, a faithful, honest, trustworthy woman, and good-tempered besides, was always to be depended upon and a great comfort to us. She still lives with members of my family.

The cook was an excellent one; but her temper was fearful, and I was dreadfully afraid of her. She is dead now, or I would not make such a confession.

In July, 1860, we were again at Fort Leavenworth, *en route* to New Mexico. "Prince John" Magruder was in command at Leavenworth that summer. I dined once with him at Fort Clark, Texas. The dinner was of necessity as plain as it could be; but it was served in courses and in grand style. John was always magnificent.

We found the usual large body of recruits and a number of officers, married and single, outward bound. My brother, then living in St. Louis, was anxious for a buffalo hunt, and went with us some distance on the Plains. Although it was to be the third time I had crossed them, I was not sorry. I really enjoyed it, although the scenery was monotonous; for weeks at a time not a tree was in sight, nothing but the green rolling prairies as far as the eye could reach.

When we left Fort Leavenworth for New Mexico, each ambulance was given its position in line according to the rank of the officer whose family occupied it; consequently, the wives and children of the lieutenants suffered much from the dust made by a long line of vehicles ahead of theirs. Meek little Mrs. Blank took it all as a matter of course, and submitted without a murmur. Not so, however, with saucy Mrs. Dash, who aired her opinions as to "rank among army women" on all occasions, and could not be made to see why the families of second lieutenants should swallow more than their allotted "peck," in a shorter time than was necessary. She thought it would be pleasant to have a day without dust occasionally, and that she would enjoy riding in front, where the carriage of the colonel was always to be seen.

It seemed to me only fair that the ambulances should change place, each taking its turn at the head of the column; but those in command did not look on it that way, and the position taken the first day out was to continue to the end.

The truth is, all army women, from the wife of the commanding general down to the wife of a second lieutenant, are treated with so much courtesy and politeness by army officers that they do not like anything that has the least appearance of a slight or an infringement of their rights. They never grow old in a garrison, and always receive attentions to which no woman in citizen life is accustomed when no longer young. I have seen gray-haired ladies at an army post dance at the hops with as much enjoyment as the younger ones, and they are always invited by the men, young and old, to do so as a matter of course. The hops are more like a family reunion than a gathering of strangers.

After Colonel Lane was retired, and we lived in the East and North, it took me some time to understand that I need not look for the numerous courtesies to which I had always been accustomed at an army frontier post, and that if I went out at all, I must join the army of "wall flowers," and expect nothing.

But I am loitering and digressing when I should be many miles on the road and in full view of the thousands and thousands of buffalo, quietly grazing and offering every inducement to the hunters to go out and kill them. The vast herds paid not the least attention to us, unless the wind blew from our direction towards them, when a regular stampede followed, and they got out of sight far more rapidly than you would believe such a clumsy, heavy beast could travel, leaving the old bulls to guard their retreat.

No wonder the buffalo has entirely disappeared from the Plains. Hundreds of thousands were killed for mere sport,—often for the tongue alone. The prairies were strewn with their carcasses, furnishing food for the roving bands of coyotes, always to be heard at night around our camps.

Those fearful storms of which I have spoken before gave us an almost daily benefit. One day our camp had been selected on a high bluff overlooking a river; Lieutenant Lane was quartermaster, and had to leave us to attend to business. We were sitting in the ambulance waiting for the tents to be pitched, and the driver was standing by his team of four fine bay mules, when a flash of lightning out of an almost clear sky, followed by a tremendous clap of thunder, sent the whole team flying along the edge of the precipice. I held on to the children and shut my eyes, expecting every instant to go over and into the river; but the trusty driver had the reins and held on with might and main, and though dragged some distance he never lost his presence of mind. He soon checked the mules, but it was a very narrow escape.

Another day, just as we got into the tent, the quartermaster was away looking after the men, when a heavy thunder-gust came up. The tent, not being well pitched, swayed with the wind, while I, with the baby in my arms, tried to steady the shaking pole. I found I could not hold it and the baby too, so I sat down on the ground to await the expected falling of the tent, the walls of which had already become unpinned. In an instant I was drenched through, as it was raining in torrents, and I leaned over the baby to keep her from drowning.

Husband arrived in the midst of the storm, and, seeing our pitiable plight, called some men to assist him, and together they held up the tent until the danger was over. The situation was amusing after the squall had passed. I must have been a funny sight, trying to keep the tent from falling. Husband laughs yet at the remembrance.

For travelling, our tent was always lined with dark green cambric, which, when there was no other shade, was a great comfort. The glare from the white canvas, with the roasting July and August sun upon it for hours, was almost unbearable; the dark lining slightly alleviated our sufferings. For weeks we barely existed in camp through the heat of the day; the tent-walls were rolled up, in hopes a stray, cool wind might find its way to us; but what came generally felt as if it had been born and raised in a fiery furnace.

Our costumes were in the Georgia style; but, like the ostrich, we felt that when our heads were hidden our bodies were invisible. No one had much inclination to watch his neighbor, nor care about his appearance; he had enough on hand trying to keep alive until the sun went down, when there was relief until next day.

Those hot prairie winds were very trying to a woman's complexion, and husband often compared the color of mine to a new saddle. I never tried but once to take care of my skin, and that was when I first crossed the Plains, going home. Some one made me a chamois-skin mask, which I put on one day and frightened the baby so badly that it is needless to say the mask was laid aside after that one trial, and I never made an effort again to preserve my complexion.

During those scorching hot days it was necessary to leave camp very early, that most of the travelling might be done in the cool of the morning. Reveille frequently sounded at two A.M., and by three breakfast was over, tents down, wagons packed, and nothing else to be done until "boots and saddles" rang out, when the recruits fell into line, officers mounted their horses, and the ladies and children crept sleepily into the ambulances, and we were off for a slow, tiresome march, the brides no doubt thinking it was not much fun after all to marry an army officer. I for one never regretted having done so, and loved every thing connected with the army: the officers,— not always the wives, however,—the soldiers, mules, horses, wagons, tents, camps, every and anything, so I was in the army and part of it.

The grass caught fire in camp one very hot day, but fortunately there was no wind, and we were able to move the ambulance and gather up many things and carry them to a safe place before the flames came close to us. Hoop-skirts were then worn, and when I heard fire call, I hurriedly replaced mine, which I had taken off in the tent, and rushed out, leaving my watch on the bed, thinking more of my appearance than of my valuables, evidently. The fire came near enough to scorch the tent-pins, but stopped right there. The damage done was slight, the loss being confined to government property. Lieutenant Lane and my brother had exerted themselves so much that the latter was overcome by the heat and unconscious for some time, but finally recovered.

Until far out on the prairies we had an abundance of excellent wood and water, but as we travelled on both became scarce. Wood was unobtainable in the treeless country through which we marched, and the only fuel was "buffalo chips." The water frequently was from a standing pool hardly fit for horses or mules, and poison almost to human beings.

One of the first things done on reaching camp was to put a guard over the water, to prevent the animals from rushing into it and making it even worse than it was.

Sometimes a train with many mules or oxen had camped there just before we arrived, and as the teamsters were not particular to keep the poor thirsty creatures out of the water, its condition beggars description, and the taste was perceptible even in coffee, which was not remarkable after droves of mules and oxen had stood in the pond for hours.

When we came to a hole of good, clean water, we filled all the kegs and a two-gallon canteen, so that we usually had enough to last us until we could get another supply just as good; but our fellow-travellers were not often as provident as we were, and many a cup of cold water we gave to those who needed it. I remember one day Lieutenant Lane was on rearguard; that is, he and the guard were at the end of the column of soldiers and wagons, with the prisoners. The day was hot, and the men were nearly wild with thirst, and mutinous. Our ambulance was also in the rear, and husband stopped it, took out all the water we had in kegs and canteen, made the men stand in line, and gave each one a good drink; they were very grateful and much cheered by it, marching quietly along until camp was reached.

FIFTEEN

I THINK IT probable you would not have enjoyed a drink
of that water from keg and canteen, as did those thirsty men.
Of course there was no ice to cool it; but the big canteen was
thickly covered with felt or piece of blanket, which was kept
constantly wet, and hung up where the breeze could reach it.
In this way the water was made quite cool; we thought it very
good indeed, scarcely missing the ice, which we could not get.

When wood was abundant we laid in a supply for future
use, carrying a log of fatty pine perhaps a hundred or two hundred miles chained under a wagon, and using it very sparingly
to kindle the fire. Any one fortunate enough to find a piece of
wood, dropped by a passing train possibly, was the envy of the
camp.

To this day, when I see a quantity of good chips lying in
the street, I can hardly refrain from gathering them up. I have
often thought if I ever become a childish old woman my delight will be to pick up sticks, remembering how valuable a
piece of wood was in a country where there were no trees.

At that time a little camp-stove of sheet-iron had been invented, which required very little wood. On top were four
holes for pots and pans, and behind the fire was a small oven
where bread could be beautifully baked and meat roasted;
there was but little weight to it, so that it could easily be
carried under the ambulance, pipe and all. As soon as camp
was reached the stove was unchained, put in position, the fire
made, and by the time the tents were ready, preparations for

our evening meal—call it what you will, dinner or supper—
were progressing rapidly, and it was not a bad one, either.

Odors from many camp-fires were soon perceptible and increased our hunger; the first noticed usually came from the
teamster's mess, and was a mixture of fried onions, bacon, hot
bread, and coffee. None of you who have not tried it can imagine with what keen relish such a simple meal was eaten; with
appetites sharpened by the pure air of the Plains, anything
tasted good, and one only asked for quantity, not quality.

Among the soldiers' wives going out to New Mexico was a
young woman whose family lived in Carlisle, and of whom I
knew something, so that I felt interested in her. She was a direct descendant of Moll Pitcher, of Revolutionary fame, whose
monument is now in a cemetery at Carlisle, Pennsylvania.

After travelling several weeks she died, leaving a baby a
few days old. The poor thing had ridden day after day in a
rough, lumbering government wagon, hard enough on a well
woman, and death, as it proved, to her. Her baby was born in
it, and there she died. Out of respect to her, we did not move
next day. A grave was dug on a little hill above the creek which
flowed through the camp, and all the officers and ladies, as well
as her own friends, followed her to her last resting-place. Lieutenant Joseph Wheeler, afterwards major-general, Confederate
States army, read the burial services at the grave. "Nature sor-
rowed o'er the scene;" black clouds hung above us, and great
drops of rain fell on the rough coffin in the open grave. Desolate enough the little mound on the hill-top looked when we
left camp early next day. Every care was taken to make it secure against the coyotes (prairie wolves), which had often
been known to tear open a grave and carry off the body. To
prevent this, large stones were placed upon it.

Years afterwards, when crossing the Plains going to the
States, I got out of the ambulance and went to the grave, which

I found undisturbed. I hoped there might be a flower growing on it, that I could take to her friends at home. I saw nothing but a few blades of grass, which I picked, adding to them some pebbles lying near, a sad souvenir to carry to sorrowing friends, revealing, as it did, the desolation of the spot where the daughter and sister was buried.

It was always a pleasure to us when going towards New Mexico to sight the Spanish Peaks, the highest of the Taos Mountains, crowned with perpetual snow. It was a change from the everlasting grass-covered stretch, which we had for weeks at a time, east, west, north, and south of us. We never seemed to get closer to the Peaks: as we advanced they receded, apparently. They were always there, grand and beautiful, in the early morning with the first rays of the sun upon them, and at evening with clouds of gold and crimson lighting up the dazzling snow on their summits.

As we approached Fort Union the appearance of the country changed: there were trees and hills to vary the landscape, and the Raton Mountains were yet to be crossed. I always enjoyed the day in the mountains; the road was not bad and the scenery was fine. A clear little noisy stream ran here, there, and everywhere, intercepting our path time and again. The crack of a teamster's big whip had a strange, muffled sound in the passes of the hills, which still rings in my ears.

Once over the Ratons, we knew our long tramp was almost done, as Fort Union was within three or four days' march of them. We might be ordered to a post hundreds of miles from Union, but we did not object to that. I liked passing through a country where we occasionally saw a house and human beings; it was less tedious than roaming over the Plains, where we never saw any one but our own command, unless we met a train of wagons returning to the States, and there was nothing very exciting in that, I am sure; but we looked after the whole long string as it passed, and were sorry when it was lost in the distance.

"The lieutenant" was ordered to remain at Fort Union, and all we had in the way of furniture, etc., was soon settled in the quarters assigned us. They were built of logs, and old, but cosey and homelike, and, with our good cook and nurse, we enjoyed housekeeping after our weeks and weeks of travel. By discreetly keeping away from the kitchen and giving as few orders as possible to the cook, the peace of the household was undisturbed. When obliged to speak to her, I made known my wants in a meek voice and beat a hasty retreat.

Some of those officers who crossed the Plains with us remained at Fort Union,—Chaplain McPheeters and family, of St. Louis, Captain "Jack" Lindsey (who resigned later and joined the Confederate States army) and wife, Dr. Bartholow and family, and several others. It was a large post, with many pleasant people whose society we did not long enjoy. We had reached Fort Union in September, and on the 22d of December we were in Santa Fé, *en route* to Fort Craig, New Mexico.

On Christmas Day, 1860, we, with several officers and their wives, dined in Santa Fé with Lieutenant Dabney Maury and wife. Some months later he joined the Southern army.

The possibility of war between North and South was freely discussed at table, with considerable excitement, and so hotly at times the ladies were embarrassed considerably. There were advocates for both sides, while others were reticent as to their sentiments. We had so little fear that matters would ever terminate seriously, and war result, that we soon forgot the unpleasant episode. But those fiercely expressed opinions and angry words were not forgotten by all who were present, and bore fruit later on; some giving up everything, believing they owed it as a duty to their native States, while others fought, bled, and died for the old flag, but that was long afterwards.

We left Santa Fé in a driving snow-storm. The day was intensely cold, and the wind, high and piercing, drove the sleet and snow into any small crevice of the ambulance that it could find unguarded. Fortunately we were not going far, and were very glad when we reached our resting-place about noon. The house was kept by an old Frenchman in a Mexican village between Santa Fé and Albuquerque. Our host had been keeping the Christmas season and "tasting his wares" very freely, so that his excessive politeness was troublesome, coming every little while to our room to know what he could do for us; otherwise we were very comfortable; and, as he seemed so happy and cheerful, we let him enjoy himself.

How well I remember the sights, sounds, and odors of the little Mexican towns! The ambulance driver always entered one at full speed, cracking his whip and urging the mules to do their best,—I do not know why, unless to impress the natives with the importance of the coming guests. The trotting of the horses of the escort, the rattle of the wagons, added to the barking of every dog in the village, bleating of terrified sheep and goats, and the unearthly bray of the ill-used burro (donkey), made a tremendous racket. And the smells! The smoke from the fires of cedar wood would have been as sweet as a perfume if it had reached us in its purity; but, mixed with heavy odors from sheep and goat corrals, it was indescribable.

I never get a whiff of burning cedar, even now, that the whole panorama does not rise up before me, and it is with a thrill of pleasure I recall the past, *scents and all.*

SIXTEEN

WHEN WE REACHED the Rio Grande, below Albuquerque, to cross, we found much ice in it, some strong enough to bear our light buggy in which I was riding with husband, and we went over safely, followed by the ambulance. The children were with the servants in the comfortable spring-wagon, which, being rather heavy, broke through the ice when the middle of the river was reached.

There it stuck fast, and in trying to pull it out one of the mules fell down and went under the ice. Great excitement followed this catastrophe; every effort was made to save the mule, but he could not get up, and at last the traces had to be cut, and he was drowned. Husband took the horse out of the buggy, mounted him bareback, rode out to the disabled wagon, and brought the children to me, one at a time. The escort, seeing the mules could not move the wagon, pulled off their shoes and stockings, rolled up their trousers, and, nothing daunted by the icy waters, without "waiting for the wagon," plunged in, and, literally putting their shoulders to the wheel, rolled it out of the hole. By much swearing, whip-cracking, and loud shouting, the three remaining mules were made to do their duty and drag the wagon across to the other side of the river.

Then the men came in for their reward, which was evidently received with much satisfaction. It was drawn from a keg, but this time it was stronger than water.

We found Mexican towns along our route where we could

stop every night. The señor from whom we rented rooms, after assuring us his poor house was at our disposal, that he was highly honored by our accepting part of it, etc., managed to get full price for all we had from him. We used our own mess-chest (doing our own cooking, usually) and beds, only needing his rooms with fireplaces to be quite comfortable. There was seldom any furniture in the room; the dirt floor was neatly covered by a woollen carpet of black and white plaid, made by the Mexicans, which, though not very gay, looked tidy. This carpeting was often woven in a most erratic fashion, and no two breadths were alike, but the colors were the same throughout: first there would come a yard, perhaps, of nicely-woven black and white check, then half a yard with stripes, followed likely by a yard of grayish-white alone, and so on all over the room; but as long as the floor had a covering, we did not object to the eccentricity displayed in the weaving of it.

Many a house at an army post had no other carpet than that made by Mexicans, and sometimes (but not often) we found a piece woven with a good deal of regularity. When soiled, it could easily be washed. Around the walls were laid wool mattresses, neatly folded and covered with gay calico; these served as seats for the Mexicans. The small, narrow, wool-stuffed pillows were there also covered with red or pink calico, over which was drawn coarse lace, like a case, with wide lace ruffles on the ends.

The walls of the rooms were a brilliant white, made so by a certain kind of earth which underwent some preparation known only to the natives, I suppose. A wash was then made of it, which was applied with a piece of sheepskin with the wool on it, perhaps because it was cheaper than a brush.

Women did the whitewashing, and they used the same material for beautifying their complexions.

The quaint little oval fireplaces were my delight, placed as they frequently were in the most inconvenient part of the room, just behind the door, perhaps, with a low wall built out between them to protect the fire from too great a draft when the door was opened. Sometimes the adobe chimney, which jutted out from the wall of the room, was washed with buff color and looked clean and pretty. A very rough and lumpy shelf, made of adobe, projected above the fireplace, and served as a mantel; but I think it would have been rather unsafe for costly ornaments, as the top was very uneven.

When the fireplaces were in a corner of the room and were full of blazing sticks of pine or cedar wood standing on end,— not crosswise, as we put them,—the effect was beautiful.

The decorations on the walls were unique, consisting of small, cheap looking-glasses and pictures of the commonest description. The glasses were hung almost at the top of the wall, in a slanting position; but they must have been for ornament only, it being impossible to see yourself in them.

The pictures were of a religious character,—of all the saints in the calendar,—horrible to see, in bright tin frames. We seldom saw any one about the houses except the person from whom we hired the rooms. They did not appear to be at all curious about us, but I think it probable we were watched by many a pair of soft, dark eyes when utterly unconscious of it.

The Mexican houses were only one story, built of adobe, with flat, dirt-covered roofs, the ceilings being of pine logs with the bark stripped off, mostly unpainted.

The windows were few and far between, and, as glass was expensive, it was not often there were more than four small panes in each one. Frequently there was no glass at all, the frame being covered with white cotton cloth; but as they opened onto a courtyard, where there was nothing to see, it made no difference, the front of the house, on the street, being only a blank wall without windows.

On the outside of the shanties hung great strings of red peppers to dry, and many a big yellow pumpkin adorned the flat dirt-roofs.

It was a rare thing to find a roof that did not leak, and it was not unusual, during the rainy season, to see on the walls of the rooms long, light-brown streaks of mud from the house-top, reminding one of a huge map of a river with its various tributaries.

When we reached Fort Craig, on the 4th of January, the same quarters were assigned to Lieutenant Lane in which we had stayed on our first visit, and where we found such a super-abundance of water. Dr. Basil Norris, U.S.A., occupied part of the house, and we were delighted to have him for our neighbor.

As the winter rolled on the war-clouds became darker, and many a serious talk we had with the doctor about the state of the country and what we would do in that far-off land in case of a crisis,—no railroads, no telegraph, and a whole month between mails. None but those who have been so situated know how terribly anxious we were. But we tried to believe affairs were not as bad as they were represented.

On the 6th of February, 1861, we were again travelling,—"the lieutenant" having been ordered to Fort Fillmore,—and I was glad to go. As there were some small settlements not far from the post, we would not feel as completely buried as we had been at Fort Craig. We were four days making the distance, eighty miles of it being across the "Jornado del Muerto" ("Journey of Death"), where there was then no water to be found.

Lieutenant Joseph Wheeler was travelling with us, having been assigned to Captain W. L. Elliott's company, stationed at Fillmore. Captain Elliott was on leave in the East.

Colonel Bomford and Captain Ewell were also of the party.

The latter resigned soon after and joined the Southern Confederacy.

Lieutenant Wheeler messed with us. I remember well one breakfast on the road. He had not then travelled enough with troops to know the necessity of an early start in the morning, and of eating rapidly, that things might be cleared away and packed in good time, with as little delay as possible.

We ate our breakfast by candle-light. Lieutenant Wheeler and I were disposed to dawdle, politely handing each other the various delicacies on the table. Lieutenant Lane finished his meal in frantic haste, and left the tent, hoping to expedite matters which were going on so leisurely within. But Wheeler did not notice husband's impatience, and it became necessary, at last, to warn us we must not waste time, that we had a long and dangerous drive before us that day, and it was getting late.

That noble and polite gentleman understood later on the necessity of haste when a march of many miles was to be made, better than he did when about to cross the Jornado del Muerto in February, 1861.

By driving far off the road water could be found, and about noon this was done. There was no path to the place, but the country was not rough enough to prevent the ambulance and wagons going to it. As we followed our leader we almost ran over the largest snake I ever saw out of a show. He was quietly sunning himself and took no notice of us. We did not resent his indifference to our approach.

SEVENTEEN

HUSBAND WAS VERY anxious to get back to the road as quickly as possible, and, after the animals were watered and would drink no more, we started to return, when it was discovered that Colonel Bomford was missing, nor could he be found anywhere in the vicinity. It was absolutely necessary for the safety of everybody and the animals to travel a certain distance each day, in a country where there was no water, so that his absence caused great uneasiness. It was a very dangerous thing for one man to leave his companions and stray away. Possibly he was so sure of his own strength he had no fears, knowing he was equal to ten Indians at least, and with Samson's weapon, the jaw-bone of an ass, he might have routed a whole tribe. He was the strongest man in the army. Late in the evening he came in leisurely, apparently quite unconcerned at our anxiety on his account. He had been quietly wandering around, amusing himself not far from where the water was found.

Most dreary and uninviting did Fort Fillmore look to us as we approached it. It was a cold, gray day, with a high wind which blew the loose sand and dust in clouds all about us. The stiff line of shabby adobe quarters on three sides of a perfectly bare parade-ground suggested neither beauty nor comfort, and for once I felt discouraged when we went into the forlorn house we were to occupy.

It was filthy, too, and the room we chose for a bedroom

must have been used as a kitchen. The great open fireplace had at least a foot of dirt in it, which had to be dug out with a spade before a fire could be lighted. It took time to make the quarters comfortable; but by hard scrubbing and sweeping they at last looked clean and habitable. The woodwork was rough and unpainted; the modern method of oiling pine was not known in army quarters then.

I was the only lady at the post except the wife of the sutler. Lieutenant Lane and Lieutenant Wheeler, and possibly one other officer, attended to all the duties of the garrison. Lieutenant Lane was in command.

There was a hospital, but no doctor nearer than forty miles, for whom we once had to send; and on another occasion the doctor at a fort eighty miles away was summoned; relays of mules were posted along the road to bring him in as rapidly as possible.

There had been no improvement in our mail facilities, and a month was still required to get letters from the East. We read with intense interest everything bearing on the subject of secession in the papers, which were a month old, when we were lucky enough to get any.

There was an undercurrent of disquiet around us which was felt more than seen or heard, and there were plenty of men in the small towns, ready at a moment's notice, in case war was declared, to make a raid on Fort Fillmore, which, with its small garrison, could offer but little resistance.

We were scarcely settled at housekeeping when an order came for all the troops to go on an Indian scout to Dog Cañon. There was nothing to be done but to obey, although everybody at the post knew there was far more danger from Texans than from Indians.

A sergeant and ten men, all that could be spared from the little command, were left behind to guard the post and our small family, and they were picked men. Those in the guard-house were taken on the scout. *I* was left in command of Fort Fillmore. All public funds were turned over to me, and the sergeant reported to me every day. He slept in our house at night, heavily armed, which gave us a sense of security.

There was a flag-staff on the parade, but no flag. Husband sent to Fort Bliss for one before he left for Dog Cañon. I knew I would feel safer to see it floating above us, and it was run up at reveille every morning through the summer before the post was abandoned. When was the flag ever more needed than in those anxious days before war was declared, to cheer the weak-hearted and bid defiance to its enemies?

The public money in my hands gave me considerable un-easiness, and I hid it away in what I considered a secure place; then it seemed to me that would be the first spot searched, and I found a safer one. I was determined no one should have that money while I was alive to defend it. Just how I would act circumstances must decide; if I lost my life in protecting it, I would have done my whole duty.

The state of affairs at Fillmore and the surrounding country had been represented at Santa Fé, and the folly shown of sending all the troops away from the post, after an imaginary foe likely, when right in our midst was a real danger to be dreaded. An express was sent to Dog Cañon with orders to abandon the scout, and, to my great joy, the soldiers returned, when, with much pleasure, I relinquished the command of Fort Fillmore. It was my first and last appearance in the role of commanding officer of a military post.

One of the small towns not far from Fort Fillmore was Mesilla, which we sometimes visited; but the Rio Grande was between us and the village, and not always in a good condition to ford, consequently we did not go very often. The Rio

Grande has of late years cut an entirely new channel for itself, placing Mesilla on the east bank, while in 1861 it was on the west side of the river.

We were invited by some friends living there to see a bull-fight; and we went, I expecting to have my blood curdle at the sight of streaming gore from matadore or bull, and to enjoy myself greatly with the horrors of the scene! But I never saw such an old, travel-stained steer tamer, nor one more unwilling to fight; no amount of red-rag waving, nor prods with iron-pointed staff, could rouse him into anything fiercer than a weary glance at his tormentor. I soon tired of such sport (?) as that, and left. I never went to see another bull-fight.

Towards the latter part of the winter the authorities at Santa Fé seemed to become aware that reinforcements were needed at Fillmore. It was but forty miles from Fort Bliss, Texas, and in case of trouble the handful of soldiers stationed there could make no resistance whatever. Major Gabriel Paul was sent to command the post, and of course chose our quarters; but when those next door were cleaned and put to rights they were as good as the house we left, and as we had little furniture to move, it was not much trouble.

The garrison was reinforced by several companies of Fifth and Seventh Infantry and Mounted Rifles, with their officers. Major Paul was succeeded by Major Lynde in the command of the post. Two doctors were sent to take charge of the hospital and sick people generally,—Doctor J. C. McKee and Doctor Alden. It was a relief to feel we need not now send one hundred miles or so, if we were ill, for a doctor.

We were turned out of quarters again that spring, but not by a ranking officer. One very warm afternoon the children and servants were playing in the yard, while we were reading in the house. Presently we heard a great commotion, and some one rushed in to tell us there "was a river at the back gate."

Husband, thinking it was a joke, dressed himself leisurely and went out, while I kept on reading. In a moment he was back to say an immense body of water was then in the yard and would be in the house in a few moments. There was no time to be lost in adorning myself, so in dressing-sack and skirt I flew round, and with the help of the servants tore up our two carpets, picked up the loose things off the floors, and soon had all articles likely to be injured by water out of the way. I don't know how we did so much in such a short time. "The lieutenant," armed with a spade, was hard at work on an adobe wall in the yard, trying to break a hole in it, to let the water escape on to the parade. I ran out the front door and beckoned to the soldiers who were seated in front of their quarters, but they took no notice. By degrees they divined something was wrong, as I kept on making motions, and they came running over to see what I wanted. I explained the situation, and they carried out the furniture as fast as possible. By the time the men arrived I was wading in water up to my knees, all over the house. Everybody, man, woman, and child, turned out to see the fun, and were amazed to see the stream that rushed through the house and out the door, spreading rapidly over the parade-ground.

The day was bright and beautiful, with not a cloud to be seen. The flood was supposed to have come from a cloud-burst in the Organ Mountains, miles away to the east of us.

The water came booming down the mountains, making right for our house; no other on the line was disturbed. Fortunately, there was a set of quarters next us vacant, so that we could go right in; this made our second move and third house at Fort Fillmore.

The quarters were not as good as others we had lived in at the post. I did not enjoy the presence of a poisonous snake in the bedroom, nor that of a bat found clinging to the sheet under which I was sleeping. I hated the bat worse than the snake, I believe. They frequently made us hurried visits; there were hundreds of bats in those old adobe walls.

EIGHTEEN

Fighting HAD BEGUN between North and South, and we were most unpleasantly situated. There were at Fillmore several officers and their families with decided Southern sentiments. One of the officers quietly retired to Texas, leaving his family to follow as best they could, showing how implicitly he relied on the chivalry of his old companions-in-arms to take care of his wife and children until they were able to join him. We knew not friend from foe.

All the little tittle-tattle of an army frontier post was treasured up and reported to Santa Fé. Silly things said on the spur of the moment were repeated and magnified into something important long after the originator had forgotten all about them. I remember on the Fourth of July, 1861, quite a number of us were singing the national airs, and some one paid a glowing tribute to the "old flag," when a sweet, gentle Southern woman made a flippant remark, at which we were all indignant. When I had her alone, I asked how she came to make such a speech. "Oh, just to tease Doctor McKee," she replied. What she said was reported at head-quarters. Many of our oldest and truest army friends resigned and went South, several of them passing through Fort Fillmore on their way out of New Mexico. Among them were General Longstreet, who came into the post driving his own ambulance, *en route* to Texas; Cadmus Wilcox, Colonel W. W. Loring, Lawrence Baker, Major Sibley, and others whose names I have forgotten. Colonel George B. Crittenden, one of our best friends, also

went down to Texas, and I never saw him again. Some left
New Mexico *via* Fort Union, crossing the Plains to reach "the
States." Much pressure was brought to bear on Lieutenant
Joseph Wheeler by his Southern relations, all urging him to
resign. Between his desire to be true to the government and
anxiety not to offend his nearest and dearest, he was almost
distracted, but he yielded at last to the importunities of his
friends and left the United States army, but very reluctantly.
Very few soldiers left the army, while in New Mexico, to join
the Southern Confederacy.

Of course, every day all sorts of rumors were brought in of
intended attacks on the post by Confederates, and caused a
good deal of uneasiness among us all. The commanding officer,
Major Lynde, seemed utterly oblivious of the danger, and took
no means to strengthen the place, nor to put his small force
where it would be most efficient in case the Texans carried out
their plans to make a raid on the garrison. Officers loyal to the
United States grew restless under Lynde's command; some
made suggestions to him as to the best manner of protecting
the post, but to all he turned a deaf ear. There could not have
been a better man in command to help the Southern cause, nor
a worse for the government, than Major Lynde.

Several alarms had been given of the advance of Southern
troops into New Mexico, and mounted parties were sent out to
investigate and intercept them, when Lynde could be brought
to see any danger that might result should the reports be true.

On one of these occasions Lieutenant Lane commanded
the troops, and I quote from an account of the affair given by
Doctor McKee, who tells it more graphically than I can:

"Lane was a hot-headed Kentuckian" (writes the doctor)
"who had his own way of being loyal, which did not suit the
extremists; but I had confidence in his determined bravery as
a soldier and his integrity as a man."

The scout left Fillmore June 22, and went down the Rio Grande towards El Paso, a rumor having been brought in that the Texans were advancing four hundred strong. First Lieutenant W. B. Lane was in command of the United States troops, and with him were Second Lieutenant C. H. McNally and Second Lieutenant E. J. Cressy, Regiment Mounted Rifles, and seventy men. The doctor says, "He (Lane) ordered his officers to examine the cylinders of each man's revolver, to see that they were properly loaded, as he intended to make it a hand-to-hand fight." . . . "Unfortunately, he did not meet the enemy"—so the doctor thought—but I was quite satisfied that they did not find "the enemy."

Just about this time I had a visit from old Charles, who had once belonged to Captain Elliot, and who took French leave while at Fort Bliss. His master came to Fillmore on business, and brought Charles with him. The old fellow was very glad to see us again, and he and I discussed the war seriously. I asked what he intended to do when the Texans reached Fort Bliss? "Get over into Mexico as quickly as possible," was his answer. "And leave old Sallie and Patsy?" (his wife and daughter) I asked. "Well," he replied, "you know the Good Book tells us to look out for number one." I was much surprised at such a reading of the "Good Book," and concluded, if he could so distort the meaning to suit his own purposes, the Mormon woman was right when she told me "the Bible, like a fiddle, could be made to play many tunes." I had said to her I did not see how the Mormons based their belief and religion on anything found in the Bible, and the above was her reply.

Late in June, or the beginning of July, the post herd was stampeded, but by whom was not known. It was suspected the friends of the Confederacy could tell a good deal about it. The stampede dismounted one or all the companies of riflemen at Fillmore, and made them foot-soldiers for the time being. Not a horse was left in the company Lieutenant Lane commanded, so that the duties of the men were curtailed, having no stable-call to attend.

About the middle of July it was decided to send some of the surplus commissary stores to Fort Craig, and the company Lieutenant Lane commanded was ordered to escort the wagon-train. Doctor McKee writes, "He (Lane) was a fighting man, and had to be got rid of."

Before leaving Fort Fillmore we sent all our furniture, china, etc., to Mesilla, to be sold at auction, and, strange to say, realized remarkably good prices for everything. We were more fortunate than those friends who remained at Fillmore and lost their all later on.

On the 24th of July, 1861, we left for Fort Craig; our escort of riflemen was distributed among the wagons, as there were no horses to ride. We had travelled but a short distance when the wagon-master insisted on halting to rest the mules, preparatory to a night march across the Jornado del Muerto, the eighty miles' stretch without water. Lieutenant Lane thought the halt so early in the day entirely unnecessary, but agreed to it, never dreaming the man had any other motive than the one given, the good of the animals. After-events seemed to prove he was playing for high stakes, but he lost, that time.

While resting I looked over the peaceful landscape, and remarked that it seemed impossible there could be war and fighting in "the States," while all here was so serene and quiet. Little did we imagine that within a very few miles of us was a large body of Texans, seriously considering the possibility of capturing the train with which we were travelling. It was filled with provisions, of which they stood sorely in need.

After resting through the heat of the day we broke camp late in the evening and started out on the Jornado, expecting to travel until about nine o'clock. It was a beautiful night, clear, and bright moonlight. Not a sound broke the intense stillness, except the slow, steady trot of the mules on the hard road. The children and servants were asleep in the ambulance, while we kept a keen lookout for danger ahead, and enjoyed the quiet all around us.

Suddenly we were roused by the noise of galloping horses coming from behind us, and in a few moments several men rode up and asked for "Lieutenant Lane." The ambulance was stopped at once, and the strangers hurriedly told their story. One of them was Doctor Steck, an Indian agent and a strong Union man, whom we had known in Mesilla. He came to warn us that two hundred and fifty Texans were ready with horses saddled to leave the lower country, overtake us that night, and capture our train! I felt as if turned to stone, and did not speak for some time. Then I asked, "What are we to do?" "Fight," answered "the lieutenant." "We will corral the wagons, use the sacks of flour and bacon for a fortification, put you, the children, and servants inside, and do our best to defend ourselves—"

Imagine my feelings! The whole number of soldiers and teamsters would not be more than sixty men all told, and the prospect of victory for our side was small. I said nothing, and tried to feel brave, but I did not—*very*.

We had heard before leaving Fillmore that Captain Alfred Gibbs, Mounted Rifles, was on his way from Albuquerque with beef cattle for that post, escorted by his company, to keep off Indians or Texans, as the case might be. If Gibbs knew of our predicament he might push on rapidly and meet us at Point of Rocks, on the Jornado, early next morning. So it was decided to send an express ahead (a man mounted on a horse) to meet him, and let him know what Doctor Steck had reported to Lieutenant Lane, and in case we did not arrive at the designated place at a certain hour, he was to come to our assist-

ance with all possible haste. I felt somewhat better after the
note to Gibbs was written—on the fly-leaf of a book, by the
light of a lantern—and despatched, but none too cheerful, I can
tell you.

Lieutenant Lane ordered the wagon-master to travel as far
and rapidly as possible that night. On we went, counting every
mile between us and our supposed pursuers as so much
gained. The moon still shone brightly on our swiftly-moving
train, and lit up the desert for miles in every direction, but not
a living thing could be seen.

NINETEEN

ABOUT ONE A.M. the report was brought to Lieutenant Lane that the mules were giving out, so we halted and camped just where we were, beside the road.

No sign of the enemy yet, and I began to breathe again and took some rest. As soon as the animals were refreshed and had grazed a little,—there was no water for them,—they were harnessed up, and we were off, hoping soon to meet Gibbs. When a cloud of dust in the distance heralded his approach, I was greatly relieved; and as help was in front and no sign of an enemy in the rear, I began to feel bold, and tried to convince myself I was not so very badly frightened after all, but I think any woman under the circumstances would have been quite as much alarmed as I was. I could not run away, lest I should meet a foe far worse than the Texans. The Indians were always somewhere in the neighborhood, so that it would have been safer to stay where we were than to fall into their clutches.

Lieutenant Lane tried to induce Captain Gibbs not to go on to Fillmore, but he decided to obey orders, taking a roundabout way to reach the post, and so avoid, he hoped, the expected enemy. That something had happened to prevent the intended attack on the wagons was evident, for, had the Texans started at the time set, they could have overtaken us hours before we met Captain Gibbs, and we heard how it was some days later.

Suspicion fell on the wagon-master for detaining us. It was

thought that he knew of the proposed capture of the train, and had delayed it on that account, that we should not get too far away to be caught. I do not know that the charges were ever proved, but appearances were strongly against him. We continued on to Fort Craig without accident or hinderance, to my great joy. Doctor Steck and those who left Mesilla with him hurried through to Santa Fé.

One morning, a few days after our arrival, we were startled by the appearance of a sergeant and two soldiers of the Rifles, whom we had left at Fort Fillmore. They had escaped capture, and made their way to Fort Craig, coming immediately to report to Lieutenant Lane, and from them we learned what took place after our departure.

What they told us of the fight at Mesilla, Major Lynde's disgraceful retreat from Fort Fillmore towards Fort Stanton, the capture and surrender of his whole command to the Texans, has passed into history; but, later, I will quote a little from Doctor McKee on the subject.

We also learned that the talked-of raid on the wagon-train, news of which was brought by Doctor Steck, was no idle rumor. It was well planned, and everything ready, when some Southern men whom we knew well, and with whom we had been friendly, implored those in command not to attempt it, "for God's sake; that there were women and children with the train!" So we were unmolested, and the Texans turned their attentions to the troops at Fort Fillmore.

Possibly the vicinity of the veterans at that post had more to do with the abandonment of the raid than any feelings of humanity there may have been for a handful of women and children.

I was writing home on the day we heard all the news from Fort Fillmore, and when my letter reached Carlisle, Pennsylvania, a month later, Colonel Andrew Porter, Mounted Rifles, was there. He was given the contents of it, and he telegraphed the news of Lynde's surrender to Washington, which was the first intimation they had at the War Department of what had taken place in New Mexico.

To quote from Doctor McKee's pamphlet, quite a large body of Confederates came up from Fort Bliss on the 24th of July, the day we left Fillmore, and it was some of these troops who were to attack the train of wagons.

Doctor McKee says, "On the night of the 24th of July, the garrison, men, women, and children, slept peacefully, with no more than the customary sentinels in time of peace, no pickets out in any direction, no precautions whatever taken to prevent surprise from the approaching enemy. Everybody seemed inert and paralyzed; yet they were all brave men, and would have done their duty, had they had a competent commander.

"The Texans, under command of Lieutenant-Colonel Baylor, to the number of four hundred men, . . . were quietly encamped within six hundred yards of the fort, intending to surprise us at daylight on the morning of the twenty-fifth, kill or capture the officers in their quarters, and then take the men prisoners in their barracks. Luckily for us, one of the Confederate pickets, composed of two old discharged soldiers, came in and alarmed the garrison, otherwise their success would have been complete, as they intended storming the place at break of day. Drums beat the long roll, the command turned out, and we were saved for the time."

The Texans crossed the Rio Grande and went into Mesilla, where they found many friends. The command at Fillmore was ordered out, and only a guard left for protection. There were between four and five hundred United States troops in all, who marched to Mesilla July 25, hoping to attack the enemy, but no attack was made. The adjutant, in the name of the commanding officer of the United States troops, demanded "an un-

conditional surrender of the forces and the town." The answer
was, "If he wished the town, to come and take it." A few shots
were fired by the Texans, which killed and wounded some of
our soldiers. Then Major Lynde ordered a retreat, and Doctor
McKee says, "Had any of the senior officers present at this time
stepped forward, put Lynde in arrest, and taken command, his
fortune would have been made."

The United States troops returned to Fort Fillmore at ten
P.M., July 25, crestfallen and indignant at the part they were
forced to play.

On the 26th Major Lynde ordered a great deal of public
property destroyed, which was done, preparatory to a hasty
retreat in the direction of Fort Stanton, New Mexico. The officers and families lost everything they owned, as they could
not take their property with them, beyond a change of clothes.
The Mexicans in the neighborhood reaped a harvest after the
soldiers left the post that night. The Texans followed up the
troops, and on the 27th the whole command was surrendered,
notwithstanding the protests of the officers. No one seemed
bold enough to place Lynde in arrest and take command. The
doctor says, "Blind, unreasonable obedience to orders (creditable always in a well-disciplined force) was the ruin of our
command."

On July 28 the Texans with their prisoners of war marched
to Las Cruces and encamped. Later they were all paroled and
ordered to Fort Union, New Mexico, preparatory to leaving
for Fort Leavenworth, Kansas.

Captain Gibbs and his company, in making a detour, fell in
with the Texans and were surrendered with the other troops.
It seemed hard that while obeying orders he should have been
so unfortunate. We were truly thankful to have escaped from
Fillmore before these events took place, and distressed that our
many friends there had suffered such humiliation. Some of the

officers and men later on had opportunities to show of what stuff they were made, and to prove their loyalty to the government, fighting with desperation born of their sufferings, brought about by their ignominious surrender so early in the war.

Major Lynde was tried and dismissed from the army; but after the war he was reinstated and placed on the "retired list." It never was proved, I believe, that he sympathized with the South, as many were inclined to think. He seemed utterly incompetent and unfitted for his important command, and it was freely discussed, after it was too late, that he was not the man for the place.

Fort Craig was not considered safe just then for women and children, and we remained but a short time. Our two colored women-servants behaved remarkably well all through our exciting march from Fort Fillmore to Fort Craig, never showing the least fear nor anxiety, nor giving trouble, and were a great comfort to us.

"The lieutenant" escorted us to Santa Fé, where General and Mrs. Canby gave me rooms in their quarters, and had a general supervision over us after Lieutenant Lane left to return to his company, still stationed at Fort Craig.

An incident happened while we were in Santa Fé which had a curious ending. One of the children had been presented, at Fort Bliss, with a handsome silver mug which had been made in Mexico. She was one day playing with it in front of the house, buried it in the sand, and left it there, I not knowing anything about it until next day. Of course it was not to be found. Notices were posted over town, and an advertisement put in the one newspaper, all to no purpose. We never expected to see it again. But nineteen years afterwards, in Washington, D.C., the cup was brought to me by a young woman, who told me her father had taken it from a Mexican in

Santa Fé, supposing it had been stolen. He put it away and had often intended to send it to us (the name was on it) , but never did until nineteen years had passed. The story was rather lame, but we excused it, as we got the cup, which we had given up as lost.

Since that time, 1861, Santa Fé has undergone many changes; there was not then a two-story house in the town, or even thought of. The cathedral, the original one, was still used, and, as we lived just opposite, we had much amusement watching the large congregation going to and coming from mass and vespers. There were no seats nor pews in the church, except possibly some chairs, provided for their own use by the few Americans who were Roman Catholics. The Mexicans knelt or sat on the hard, cold floor of tiles or brick during the entire service.

TWENTY

THE MEXICAN WOMEN still wore the national dress, which suited them much better than the half-American and wholly bad style recently adopted by them. Many of the fancifully adorned señoritas walked to church in satin slippers, frequently dispensing with stockings altogether, which was not a bad arrangement, perhaps; for, if the beauty of her dainty shoes was endangered by the ankle-deep dust in the streets, she could easily take them off and go barefooted without exciting comment from the passers-by, but dust more or less did not seem to trouble them.

When the bells rang out on Sunday, announcing the end of morning service, circus wagons filled with a band and the actors were sure to pass the church, as a reminder of the performance to take place later in the day, and which part of the congregation was certain to attend between mass and vespers.

The yard around the cathedral had been used as a cemetery for two hundred years, and was more than full. Often, in digging a grave, a human skull or bone was thrown out, but it caused little excitement, happening so frequently.

At a child's funeral a band headed the procession, playing the gayest music. I asked why only children's funerals were attended by a band? "Because," said my informant, "when a child dies we rejoice that it has escaped so much sorrow and has surely gone to heaven, while with older people—" a very suggestive shrug just here intimated in that case the matter was doubtful, and that rejoicing might be somewhat out of place.

I saw a funeral once at Las Cruces, New Mexico; the priest with his book headed the procession, and there were several men playing violins. The rear was brought up by friends who fired their revolvers occasionally, "to drive the devil away," they explained. I suppose nowadays, with the influx of an American population, all this is changed, and the Mexicans bury their dead in true regulation style.

I was told in Santa Fé that a coffin was seldom put into a grave; that the body was carried to the church in one, but before burial was removed, rolled in an old blanket, and consigned to the tomb. The reason was, coffins were too expensive and scarce for poor people, and were looked upon as a luxury far beyond their means, so that one was only used for show. Speaking of the difficulty of procuring a coffin reminds me that at a frontier post it was often impossible to get enough new lumber to make one, when there was a death among officers or soldiers, and old packing-boxes had to be brought into requisition. An officer died at a post in Texas, and nothing could be found for a coffin but some old commissary-boxes, which were hastily put together, and the poor fellow was carried to his last resting-place in a very rough one, on which was marked, in great black letters, "200 lbs. bacon!"

Indians were to be met with in the streets of Santa Fé constantly, both Pueblos and Navajos, who went there to trade. I found a Navajo chief one day with a little basket for sale, which I was anxious to buy, offering him money for it, but he would not take it. He wanted beads, and I bought him some, with which he was delighted, and I got my basket, which I have used constantly ever since.

Early in the fall it was decided to send the paroled troops from Fort Union to Fort Leavenworth, Kansas; and husband, who was again ordered from Fort Craig to Union, thought I, with the children and servants, had better join them. Matters in New Mexico being in a very unsettled state just then, women and children were in the way, so we left for the East with the officers and families going in. "Captain Lane," it was then, travelled with us several days to get us well started on what was to be my fourth trip across the Plains. As it would be cold before we reached Leavenworth, he had a small stove put into the spring wagon, which had been comfortably fitted up for our use, and in which we were to travel.

Our ambulance had been sold to good advantage before we left Fillmore, and the wagon, being roomy, answered very well. In addition to the one used as an ambulance, we had a government wagon for baggage and tents, of which we had two,—one for ourselves and the other for the servants, used also for a cook tent.

Husband travelled with us as long as he could be away from his post, when he put us under the care of Captain Joseph Potter, who had been with us at Fillmore, and went back to Union. Time rolled on as monotonously as usual, one day so much like another we hardly knew when the weeks began or ended.

As we were travelling east, the Spanish Peaks were behind us, and now our anxiety was to have them disappear. It was with a feeling of relief we looked back to find them no longer visible; it seemed as if we were really making headway when the last vestige of their blue summits, touched here and there with snow, had vanished below the horizon, and the familiar landmark was gone!

I never expected then to see the Peaks again, but they have loomed up before me in all their majestic beauty several times since those memorable days, but always from the window of a Pullman sleeper.

I never saw men sadder nor more disheartened than the officers of the Fifth and Seventh Infantry with whom I crossed the Plains in 1861. Some of them saved their ambulances when they left Fort Fillmore, so that their families were comfortable so far; but they had not been able to carry away more than a change of clothes, and were in a sorry plight.

Major Lynde and his wife were with the paroled troops, but had no intercourse with the officers and their families.

By the middle of October the nights in camp were very cold, and it was far from pleasant rising at daybreak, and even before, breakfasting by candle-light, and being miles on the road by sun-up. As we approached the end of our march (there were still two weeks more of it before we could reach Leavenworth), I began to wonder how I could dispose of my wagon and camp equipage when done with them. The problem was solved for me, almost as soon as I began to think of it, in a disagreeable and unexpected manner. I will tell you about it.

We were travelling slowly as usual one day, in a perfect gale of wind, a Kansas wind, which whirled the light dust in every direction and almost blinded us. It was cold, too, and we longed to get under the tents, that we might be protected from the chilly blasts and rolling clouds of dust.

When the camp was selected, we found it was on a high bluff overlooking a creek. The grass was very tall, dry as powder, and quite as inflammable, so much so that I was alarmed at the thought of lighting fires near it, and so informed Captain Potter, who came up to choose a place for our tents. He allayed my fears by telling me that even should a fire start we would be entirely out of its way, and I supposed he knew whereof he spoke.

The tents were pitched, and everything required for the night was put into them, beds made, etc. I had just gone into mine, when I heard an unusual noise, and I went to the door to see what caused it. Will I ever forget the scene before me? The grass was on fire, and the flames, driven by the wind, leaped a hundred feet at a time! It was a fearful sight. I knew instantly our only safety was in flight, and not a second must be wasted. As I left the tent, I seized such of the bedclothes as I could reach, and threw them outside; took one child in my arms, and the other by the hand. The servants followed, and by this time every woman and child in the camp had joined us. We fled down the side of the hill and into the water, which was nearly knee-deep, the poor little children bravely struggling beside us,—those that could walk,—then up the opposite bank, never looking back until we had the water between us and the fire. All the officers and soldiers ran as soon as it started, to try to beat it out with blankets, and even their coats, but that was impossible.

The light, blazing grass was carried in every direction by the high wind, and nothing could be done to check the fury of the flames. As we dumbly watched the scene, great burning weeds leaped across the creek, so close to where we stood that we were bewildered by our dangerous position.

The officers, finding all their efforts to control the now wide-spread conflagration were thrown away, and seeing how helpless we were, came to our rescue at once. They guided us down the hill to the road where it crossed the creek, and we waited there until it was safe to return to camp, or what was left of it. There were but few of the officers' tents left, and, if it had been planned to burn ours, the purpose could not have been better carried out. The fire came straight towards them, and nothing was left in our pretty camp but one big wagon and the running-gear of the ambulance.

Only the irons that had been on the ends of the poles were to be seen of our tents. Beds, table, chairs, mess-chest, everything we had for camping was gone. All our warm wraps, shawls, furs, etc., not in daily use and put into the tent at night, were carried in the ambulance for convenience, besides various articles of clothing for the children, new shoes, etc. All shared the same fate; not a vestige was left of any of them but a pile of ashes, which was soon scattered broadcast by the tempest. Desolation was on every side; the whole country was black with the remains of the burned grass.

The fire started on the opposite side of the camp from where our tents stood. A soldier cooking for an officer's family, wanting to get rid of the tall weeds, stuck a lighted match into them, and in a second everything in the vicinity was ablaze; our friends lost nothing, the wind blowing away from them, but the flames swallowed up everything in their path. Fortunately, the commissary train was out of the way and escaped the destruction which fell so heavily on some of us, not half as well able to bear it as Uncle Sam.

When I left my tent so rapidly at the first alarm, I forgot entirely the small trunk, which was put into it always as soon as we reached camp. I carried in it all the money I had, which was precious little, and other valuables.

While I was sadly contemplating the ruin around us, I suddenly discovered my box right beside me, and on top of it the blankets and pillows were piled which I had seized and thrown out of the tent. Neff, our faithful man and a discharged bugler who stayed about the wagons, was more thoughtful than I, and when I left he gathered up what he could and carried all to a place of safety until the fire had exhausted itself. When Captain Lane was about to leave us and return to Fort Union he told Neff, the last thing, to keep an eye on that trunk, no matter what happened, and the good soul obeyed orders strictly.

TWENTY-ONE

THE OUTLOOK FOR COMFORT during the next two or three weeks was anything but cheering. It was more serious than amusing to be left without wraps or warm clothing at that season of the year. The trunks in the wagon were not injured, but there was nothing in them suitable for camping. I found a fancy woollen hood for myself packed away, and, as all my hats and bonnets were burned, I was glad to have it. A new blue flannel blouse, such as the soldiers wore, was given to me, and a friend gave one of the children an overcoat, too small for her boy, which answered very well. Our supply of bedclothes was very small. I had only succeeded in saving two blankets and a pair of pillows. Two sheepskins were also snatched as brands from the burning, and played a conspicuous part in the making of our bed for some weeks. I do not remember now where we found blankets for the servants; perhaps from the quarter-master, who, as a rule, is none too generous with his goods and chattels.

I had no time to wonder where a tent for us was to come from: the bachelor officers gave up their "Sibley" at once for our use, while they, generous fellows, stowed themselves away in one hardly large enough for three men, and there were six or seven of them to be accommodated. Among them were Captain Joseph Potter, Lieutenant F. J. Crilly, Lieutenants Hancock and Ryan (both killed in the late war) , and Doctor B. J. D. Irwin.

How we were to travel for the next few weeks was a question. Our spring-wagon had gone up in smoke, and those who had ambulances had plenty to fill them. Nothing could be found but one of the great big ten-mule wagons, used for hauling commissary stores or corn. The load was taken out, except a few sacks of grain, which were left to serve as seats. I must say I have ridden on softer ones.

Many of the ladies and children had all the clothes they owned destroyed by the fire, and it was no easy matter to supply their wants from the depleted wardrobes of those who, although not quite destitute, had lost much, but we all gave something.

After the destruction of our camping "outfit," having no table nor chairs, our meals were served upon, not the green, but the brown sward; it was too late in the year for green grass. To eat them we were obliged to sit on the ground, pleasant enough on a hot day in the country for one meal, but by no means agreeable for a constancy in cold weather. I think I had too much of it, for ever since that experience I have despised picnics and out-of-door entertainments.

The servants occupied the tent with us, and fared as well as we did for a bed, which was not as soft and luxurious as some upon which I had slept. We reposed upon the bosom of mother earth. For the one which the children and I used, the two sheepskins were laid down, and then the pillows. We covered up with the two blankets and various odds and ends.

One evening the front of the tent was thrown open, and the bed just made up was in full view, when Captain Potter came to ask if I needed anything for the night. He could not help seeing it, and asked, with a twinkle in his eye, if that was where we slept? Our bed was sumptuous compared with those some of the officers had, but they never spoke of them. The nights were cold, and often the frost glistened and sparkled on the white canvas walls by the light of a candle.

In the early morning, while the men took down the tents and loaded the wagons, we all gathered about the camp-fires and compared notes as to the experiences of the past night, and how we twisted and turned to dodge a root or an extra hard spot on the ground, but one and all made light of the discomfort, and no complaints were heard.

Our wagon was so high that a good deal of skill was necessary to get in and out of it. When we were all inside, and the "tail-board" was put up, it was thought impossible for us to get down without help, and that we were safe until camp was reached; but I proved to my friends that it took something higher than a big wagon to hold me, if I wanted to get out.

We were moving sleepily along the road one day, when four mules attached to an ambulance dashed past us and across the prairie at full speed. In a few moments the bolts that held the body to the wheels loosened, and over it went to the ground. The wife and children of Lieutenant Stivers were in it, and no one was near to go to their assistance but me; so I climbed out of the front of the wagon somehow, and was first at the scene of the disaster. I feared I knew not what, but there was no tragedy in the tableau that met my anxious eyes; such a mixture I never beheld! As soon as I discovered there were no broken bones, the comic side of the picture presented itself, and I took in the situation at a glance.

Mrs. Stivers, the children, bottles of milk, contents of lunch-basket, and numerous other articles were piled together in a heap, and it was some moments before the human part could be dragged from the débris. When the officers, riding far ahead with the column of troops, heard of the accident, they came back to see what had happened, and after they found nobody was hurt, they asked, in astonishment, how I got out of my two-story wagon? I did not tell them, nor would I accept

offers of help to return to it, but managed beautifully by myself—when no one was looking.

The broken ambulance was soon repaired, and we continued on our march. A more forlorn party of United States
troops, women, and children never entered Fort Leavenworth
than that with which I travelled in 1861. We were all shabby
together, and strongly resembled a band of gypsies or travel-
stained emigrants when we arrived.

Our camp was right beside one occupied by a Western
volunteer regiment waiting to take the field—*or anything else.*
A very rough set of men indeed, and not at all agreeable as
neighbors.

We left Leavenworth on a boat. There was part of a regiment of Iowa soldiers, bound I know not where, on board, and,
as we crossed the gang-plank, a crowd gathered to gaze at us.
We felt as if we were part of a show, and we certainly must
have been an odd sight in our motley garments and sun-and-
wind-burned faces. As we stepped on to the boat, one of the
crowd exclaimed to his companions, "Here come the old
Revoluters!" And I have no doubt we looked as if we belonged
to the last century.

When I went to my state-room that night I found a man
already in it. Some mistake had been made, and it had been
assigned to both of us. Again the officers came to my relief,
kindly giving up one of their rooms to us, while they calmly
lay down on the cabin floor and went to sleep. They had not
been much pampered for some weeks in the way of sleeping
accommodations, and found the warm floor better than "the
cold ground" on which they had reposed for many a night. But
the new soldiers were not as well pleased with their resting-
place as my friends were, apparently, for I heard one exclaim,
next morning, after lying on the floor all night, "Ah! this *is*
roughing it!" I have no doubt the poor fellow had occasion

many times to look back to that comparatively comfortable night, and wonder how he ever could have thought he was "roughing it" when sleeping on the floor of a steamboat; but the war was only a few months old then, and what was considered a trial at that time was luxury later on.

We left the boat for railroad cars of the poorest and most uncomfortable kind, not anything like as good as the emigrant cars of to-day, but we thought them rather fine after our recent experiences on the plains.

St. Louis was safely reached, and there we were to part from the friends with whom we had travelled so far, and make our way East alone. We remained a few hours at the Southern Hotel to prepare for the trip and receive the passport then necessary before we could leave the city.

I had discharged my cook at Fort Leavenworth, and her services were gladly secured by a lady as nurse. So my party was reduced to myself, two children, and nurse.

While at the hotel a young man came to me with a printed form, on which he wrote a general description of my appearance, color of eyes, hair, height, and age. I was too young then to object to questions on that usually tender point.

I took an oath not to give aid nor comfort to the enemy, etc., all of which I promised, without reading what was required of me. I supposed it was a mere matter of form, and did not examine the paper until some time after the man had left. I was not likely to be placed in a position "to give help to our enemies," and I should have signed anything bearing on that subject; my whole object was to get away from St. Louis as soon as possible, and I thought everything was settled.

TWENTY-TWO

THROUGH MY IGNORANCE and the carelessness of the man who issued the passport, we came near having a serious time in leaving the city. He did not ask if there was anybody with me for whom another was required, and it had not occurred to me to mention my colored nurse, thinking one paper sufficient.

When we reached the ferry-boat I found all my baggage, trunks, chests, etc. on board, and felt happy at the prospect of starting in a few moments. I was asked for our passports. I handed my only one to the man, and said, quietly, I had no other. Then there was a scene! He was a brute, and rough and insolent to me, and there was not a soul to protect me from him whom I knew. None of my friends could take me to the boat, as they were going in a different direction, and I had to fight for myself. I stated the case as plainly as I could, all to no purpose. He declared the girl should not leave unless she had a passport also, and seemed to work himself into a rage over the matter, for some unknown reason. The passengers gathered around me and expostulated with him. The time was up for the boat to start, and I was in despair, imploring him to let us go. A quiet, handsome man, evidently a distinguished person, moved by my distress, stepped forward with his passport, and asked if the name on it would not carry the lady over. "No," was the answer. Finally some one in authority on the boat, who had been watching the exciting scene, came up, and, asking for my passport, wrote upon it, "Vouched for by H. Q. Sanderson." Who he was I never knew, but his signature was sufficient to carry us over the river, and I thanked him as well as my agitation would permit. I still have that passport.

The gentleman who had tried to take us across the ferry on the strength of his name travelled with us for two or three days, never intruding, and seemingly taking no notice of us until some assistance from him would be agreeable; then he would come forward, pick up bundles and baskets, carry them to another train, put them in place, and retire to his own seat. And I let that man leave the cars without finding out who he was, which I have never ceased to regret, as I was most grateful to him for his kindness and his thoroughly respectful manner towards me. I was young and shy in 1861, and disliked to approach a stranger and ask his name.

When we reached Harrisburg, Pennsylvania, whom should I find waiting for us but Captain Lane? He had left New Mexico in the overland stage, and was in the East weeks before we arrived. He had applied to General Canby for a leave, which was refused. His object was to go to Kentucky, where a cavalry regiment had been raised, and the command of it offered to him. He wanted to go to Washington and ask permission to take it, so when his leave was refused there was nothing to do but to resign, which he did, going immediately to Washington, where he withdrew his resignation and requested that he might accept the colonelcy of the Kentucky Union cavalry regiment. The authorities would not grant his petition, but ordered him to proceed to Philadelphia and assist Colonel Charles Ruff in mustering Pennsylvania regiments.

Afterwards he was made chief mustering and disbursing officer for Pennsylvania, and stationed at Harrisburg and Philadelphia until the close of the war.

We had been home but a few days when one of the children became ill with scarlet fever. As the only house we had been in between Fort Union, New Mexico, and Carlisle was the hotel in St. Louis, I suppose that is where the disease was contracted, or on the cars, possibly. Hers was the only case.

I had not been East long before I discovered that, to be considered "truly loyal," I must give up all kindly feeling towards our old army friends who had gone South, and that such sentiments must be eradicated at once. I could not hate them, no matter how much I opposed and disliked their opinions; so, as my poor convictions could neither carry on nor end the war, and were not necessary for the good of the country, I kept them to myself, and thus avoided squabbles and political discussions, which I detested, and of which I knew nothing whatever.

We remained East all through the war,—those years so full of anguish for our whole country.

In 1863 I had the most serious illness of my life, pneumonia, and for six weeks the chances for life or death were about even, but I did not die, you see.

It was not until the summer of 1866 that we returned to the frontier, and I was glad New Mexico was again to be our station. We had great difficulty in securing servants to go with us, but at last hired a very homely middle-aged white woman, who professed to know everything about cooking. A young English girl who was almost worthless went with us as nurse for a baby boy who had been added to our small family.

At Fort Leavenworth, Captain McNutt, of the ordnance, invited us to stay at his house while we remained. It was very kind of him, for a family of seven, added to his small bachelor establishment, made a good deal of difference.

Captain McNutt was well known in the army for his absent-mindedness, and many funny stories were told of him. One I heard in Texas was quite characteristic of the man. It was noised abroad that a grand entertainment was soon to be given by Captain McNutt, and everybody was on the *qui vive* for an invitation. Preparations were made on a grand scale, the supper was ordered, and on the night of the party the house was brilliantly illuminated, the captain in full dress, only awaiting the coming of his guests to be perfectly happy. But they never came! He discovered before the evening was over not an invitation had been sent out: they were lying in his desk, where he had placed them after they were written!

We found a number of officers and their families at Fort Leavenworth under orders for New Mexico; my fifth journey it was to be. There were no less than six brides in the party, and not a woman among all those going out had ever crossed the Plains but me, and I am certain a good many were not pleased at the prospect before them. We had made every preparation possible for our comfort and convenience. A fine large ambulance, used by General Sheridan in the valley of the Shenandoah, and sold by the government after the war, held the entire family. We had a buggy, too, which we called the "Mother's Refuge," into which I retreated when I wanted rest and quiet.

A very high horse, purchased at a very low price, served to amuse the children, and they were sometimes allowed to ride him. He was entitled to be a namesake of Big Foot, the Sioux chief, for such hoofs I never saw before. As he was not bought for speed nor beauty, he answered very well, and old "Ned" is remembered most kindly to this day by the younger members of the family.

It was amusing to an old campaigner like myself to see the brides start off from Fort Leavenworth for an ambulance expedition of six hundred miles. Their dainty costumes were far more suitable for Fifth Avenue than camp and a hot, dusty ride in the broiling sun day after day. They awoke to the fact very soon. Hoops were fashionable then, and a good deal of manœuvring was required to get in and out of an ambulance with ease, not to mention grace. Some of the ladies wore little turbans with mask veils and delicate kid gloves.

I started out as I intended to dress throughout the march,—a calico frock, plainly made, no hoops, and a sun-bonnet, and indeed I must have looked outlandish to my young friends just from New York, but there was not a husband who did not commend my common-sense dress, urging their wives to adopt it. Many of them did, in a short time, and admitted they were more comfortable, even though the change was not becoming.

Such an expedition to the uninitiated, especially when the heart was not in it, was exceedingly wearisome. The necessity for early rising was a trial in itself. Many were unable to eat the breakfast served while the morning star still shone in the heavens. A cup of hot coffee, hastily swallowed, was all they required, but I, from long practice, had learned to enjoy my breakfast at three A.M. as much as at a later hour.

While we were despatching the early repast by the light of a candle, the cook baked pans of biscuit and fried quantities of bacon and any fresh meat obtainable. All this was put into a large tin box, provided especially for the purpose. Sometimes a huge, and undoubtedly very poor, dried-apple pie was added, and that was a feast indeed, and I assure you Delmonico never served a luncheon that was more enjoyed than those of which we partook, not at the conventional hours of one or two P.M., but generally at seven or eight *A.M.* I must not forget the canteen full of tea, the outside of which was kept wet, making the contents agreeably cool. Delmonico's guests would possibly prefer something stronger than tea; but of one thing I am certain, few of them would have the same enjoyment from their fine wines that we had with our cold tea, the pure air of the plains adding a zest to our humble fare and mild beverage. I do not say there was not "a stick" added sometimes on occasion.

TWENTY-THREE

FREQUENTLY THE INDIANS made us visits after we reached camp. They seemed to pop up most unexpectedly; and though we could not see one while riding along the road, we had no sooner turned into camp than they suddenly swooped down upon us like a swarm of locusts. They were utterly regardless of time and season, making the calls as it suited their own pleasure and convenience. They came close up to the tent, staring at us, no matter in what state of undress we might be. Our dishabille, however, was full dress, compared with their visiting costumes. A regular dandy honored us one day, and this is what he wore: an army officer's coat, well buttoned up, an old sword dangling from a leather belt, a soldier's cap, and moccasins; no sign of trousers nor leg-covering had he, and he seemed utterly unconscious of the absence of those garments deemed so essential in the presence of ladies and polite society. He bore himself with becoming dignity, no doubt being perfectly satisfied with his appearance.

Quite a serious accident happened to the wife of Lieutenant James Casey, after we had been out for some weeks. The driver of her ambulance went to sleep, and, of course, did not see a small hill over which the road, ran; and the mules, being left to their own devices, made too short a turn, upsetting the carriage. Husband saw the mishap, and before I knew what had happened he threw the reins to me and ran to give what assistance might be required. The poor little woman was found to be in great agony, and was lifted with difficulty. A halt was made, and everything done for her relief by the surgeon with the command. Several ribs were broken, and she was badly bruised and sprained. When she was made comparatively comfortable, we travelled on to camp.

Think how she suffered, carried along in the ambulance day after day; she could not be left, as there was no house for hundreds of miles, and if one had been found she would have had no doctor; travel she must, even though it killed her. But she did not die, though it was months before she was able to walk about.

The army woman of to-day has no idea of the hardships so patiently endured by her mother (in the army, also). She now makes her trips from ocean to ocean in six or seven days, while the mother travelled at a snail's pace for weeks to accomplish one-quarter the distance. If this young woman rides twenty-five or thirty miles in an ambulance from the railroad to the post where her husband is stationed, she arrives completely exhausted and imagines herself a heroine. The mother was forced to travel with the command, sick or well, while if the younger woman is indisposed there are numbers of very pleasant towns or ranches along her route where she can tarry for a few days until she recuperates, or she can be quite comfortable in a Pullman car.

I recollect once, when I was crossing the Plains, a baby was born to the wife of one of the officers with the command. Next day she rode eighteen miles in her ambulance, doing the same thing daily until we arrived at Fort Union, New Mexico. And I knew another young wife whose baby was born in a tent in the wilds of Texas, far from any post or settlement. Having no woman to give her the care she required nor to tell her what was necessary to be done, she became totally blind from the glare of the sun on the white canvas walls. I met her afterwards, and she was but a shadow of her former self. It was pathetic to see her groping about from room to room in that soft, gentle way peculiar to those who have not always been blind. Her baby died.

Think of what I have told you, my young army friends, and cease to grumble at trifles. Compare your lot with your mother's, and see how much more comfortable you are than she was. She liked pretty things and luxuries as much as you do, but had very few of either, and she was quite as handsome and young, too, as you are when she gave her heart and hand to the fascinating Second Lieutenant Buttons, who endowed her "with all his worldly goods," which usually meant his monthly pay of from sixty-eight to ninety dollars a month, and some bills—tailor bills—for clothes, which helped to make him so irresistible. Her bridal tour was to a frontier post, a thousand miles from anywhere, and a journey of a month or six weeks between her and her old home.

So be content, my dears, with all your advantages, your pretty homes and your good husbands. I know they are good; all army men are, or ought to be.

While making speeches I have left the Santa Fé trail far behind, and I must hurry to the crossing of the Arkansas River. It was booming when we reached it, and had overflowed its banks. It was too high to ford, so that we were delayed until the waters subsided. We longed to get to the other side of the ugly yellow stream, narrow, yet very deep, and we cast many an anxious glance at the angry, foaming flood. Much time was spent testing its depth, until finally it was thought with extreme care we might cross. A rope was stretched from bank to bank by which the men could steady themselves, the current being swift and dangerous.

Everybody and everything passed over without accident,

when a handsome young German corporal, disdaining the rope, started to swim to the other shore, plunging fearlessly into the water. In a moment he disappeared, and was not seen for some time; but as Colonel Lane rode into the river the body came up, face downward, and was carried right by the horse. It was secured and taken ashore, where everything was done to restore life, but without avail. The man had been sick for some days in the hospital, and it was supposed he was too weak to endure the exertion of swimming across the river.

It was very late when camp was reached that afternoon. Preparations were at once made for the funeral, a grave dug, etc. It was dark when all was ready. The mournful procession, headed by the drum and fife and men carrying torches, was as touching a sight as I ever witnessed, as it passed on its way to the spot selected for the burial,—the solemn stillness of the night broken only by the steady tramp of many men to the music of the dead march.

It was awful to think of that man, so full of life but a few hours before, being hurried into a lonely grave far from home and friends.

The funeral party returned to camp marching to the jolliest airs played on drum and fife, and the handsome German soldier shared the fate of millions,—was forgotten.

To have seen the oceans of tears shed by my homely maids at the funeral, one might have imagined he was their nearest and dearest; possibly it was nervous excitement which caused the unusual overflow.

We had travelled along the Arkansas for several days before we forded it. There was once an old trading-post on the river known as "Bent's Fort." I recollect seeing a man about the place who had been more than scalped by the Indians. It was seldom one survived that operation, but this fellow was an exception, and was lively enough, although his head was still bandaged. His recovery was almost miraculous, for the whole skin had been torn from his head, from ear to ear, back and front. I take it he hoped to live to meet his red brethren again, that he might do unto them as they had done unto him. There was not much love in those days between a frontiersman and an Indian, and there is not a great deal even now.

As we approached New Mexico a certain unrest seemed to take possession of everybody, and there was a good deal of excitement visible as the old, well-known points of interest rose up before us.

Fisher's Peak was one that I loved, and is near the now flourishing town of Trinidad, Colorado. We remember when there was but one house in the place. Our recollections of that little Mexican jacal are vivid, for husband had occasion to go into it, and when he returned to camp I found something crawling on his coat which I will not name.

Our tents were pitched in full view of Fisher's Peak in 1866, and we remained a day in the pretty camp. A soldier drew a picture of it for one of the children, which is still in my possession. Our own tents, wagons, ambulance, and buggy made a little village by themselves, and I have a feeling of homesickness when I look at my picture.

There was certainly something fascinating in the roving life we led that exactly suited me, but I am confident many of our companions on that journey congratulated themselves when it was over; and as it was their first experience in that kind of travelling, it was not remarkable they were somewhat weary, and looked forward with pleasure to the day when we should arrive at Fort Union. Many of those with whom we crossed the Plains in 1866, and knew so well, are long since dead; some I never heard of again, while others we meet occasionally.

Among the officers and families were General Sykes, in

command, Colonel "Pinky" Marshall and wife, Colonel Henry
Bankhead and wife, Lieutenant Newbold and wife, Lieutenant James Casey and wife, Lieutenant Ephraim Williams,
Lieutenant Granville Lewis, and many others whose names
have escaped my memory.

TWENTY-FOUR

W E WERE MUCH AMUSED at a speech made by a pretty bride when the march was done. We were talking it over, when she remarked that she thought her father would enjoy such a trip, and added, "He is an *older man* than you, Colonel Lane." Such a speech was like a dash of cold water in your face, if you were not old and did not consider yourself so. She evidently thought Colonel Lane almost too infirm to travel so great a distance.

But he had his revenge. He met her, a grayhaired matron, a few years ago in Washington. His remaining locks were untouched by Father Time, and were still brown. He reminded her of her speech, and they had a hearty laugh about it and other incidents of the journey.

At Fort Union we remained several weeks, camping in a house, and awaiting assignment to a station. Great anxiety was displayed by the new arrivals regarding the posts in New Mexico,—where they were, if pleasant, etc. One day several of the ladies who had just crossed the Plains were at our quarters, when General Pope called. Of course they asked him where he was going to send their husbands. He, without answering, inquired of each one separately where she would like to go, and they told him, selecting, of course, the posts of which they had heard the best accounts.

When he asked me, knowing how useless it was to make a choice, I replied, indifferently, it made no matter to me where we were stationed. I was not going to say which post I preferred, for it was not probable we would be sent anywhere near it. When orders came for Colonel Lane to proceed to Santa Fé and take command of Fort Marcy, my friends were mad with envy, and one of them remarked, "That is your reward for keeping your mouth shut." Of course the likes and dislikes of the wives were not taken into consideration, nor even remembered, when their husbands were assigned for duty at a post.

The four days we spent on the road between Fort Union and Santa Fé were very depressing and disagreeable: it rained without intermission, and camping on the wet ground was most uncomfortable. Our bedding was far from dry, and there was a damp, chilly feel in the tent that made us shiver. A quantity of fresh, clean hay laid over the canvas floor-covering helped matters somewhat, and a pan of hot coals warmed the air a little. The tent was one left over from the war, and by no means water-tight.

A dismal little stream trickled through it on to the foot of the bed, over which was laid a rubber blanket, to prevent it from being saturated and to turn the rivulet from the bed to the ground.

It was, indeed, a miserable experience, and my powers of patience and endurance were taxed to the utmost. I think I would then have sold at a low rate any future chance I might have to camp out.

The day before we reached Santa Fé our baby became ill suddenly. It was fortunate for us that a ranch was not far from camp, where we were able to rent a room for the night. The house was famous at that time as a stopping-place in the beautiful "Glorietta Cañon," where we could be quite comfortable. Any house was better than a tent in such a rainstorm, and with a very sick baby to be cared for we were grateful for the refuge. As he seemed a little better next day, we decided to continue on to Santa Fé, where we arrived early in the afternoon, going at once to Fort Marcy.

The fort was very small, and just on the outskirts of the town. The quarters, built of adobe, were miserable, leaky, and in a tumble-down condition generally.

We made ourselves as comfortable as we could be in such a poor house, but we were so anxious about the baby that there was no time to worry over trifles. There were two excellent army doctors at Fort Marcy, who were untiring in their attentions to him; he was ill unto death for days, but, through their watchful care, he was given back to us from the brink of the grave. It is only necessary to add that the doctors were J. Cooper McKee and David L. Huntington, and hundreds of their patients will understand that there was nothing left undone that could afford the child relief or assist us in our care of him.

Our housekeeping at Santa Fé was an up-hill business; only one of the servants we had taken out with us remained. The cook, ugly as she was, won the hand—I cannot say the heart—of a stone-mason at Fort Union, almost immediately,—how, I never understood. She was old as well as ugly, and not at all pleasant-tempered, and, to crown all, a wretched cook. When she was disagreeable, she always showed it by reading her Bible,—always a sure sign of ill temper with her. The man must have needed a housekeeper badly to marry old Martin.

The nurse took her place in the kitchen, and I had to teach her everything. I was more capable then than when I undertook to instruct Mike, the Irishman, in the art of cooking. We managed not to starve. We had cows which gave us all the milk and butter we required, I doing all the butter-making myself. A great deal of the milk I gave to the soldiers stationed at Marcy, and also sent it to my neighbors, who had none. I remember my indignation when an officer, who had not been long in the army, asked me to sell him some, and the wife of an officer, whose baby I had supplied with new milk, sent to me for her bill!

I was very fond of Santa Fé, and enjoyed living there,—the old place was so far behind the times. The strange customs of the people and the funny sights we saw would amuse you, but I cannot well go into particulars. Fandangos and balls were of nightly occurrence. I had heard so much, and been told so often, of the great beauty of the Mexican belles who graced the dances with their presence that I determined to see them. We made up parties of ladies occasionally, and under the escort of several officers went to look on; but we were always unfortunate, and never succeeded in seeing the beauties. They were unavoidably absent when we were there, and I have the first really pretty Mexican woman yet to see. I think much of their beauty lay in their dark eyes, which they knew how to use on the poor deluded men, while in talking to a woman they kept them modestly cast down. The sweet voices, whispering soft Spanish nothings, completed the conquest, and by the time the party was over every man there, married and single, was willing to swear to the exquisite beauty of Señorita Blanco and the bewitching grace of Señorita Dulce.

When their raptures were coldly received by us,—the women critics,—they were amazed at our indifference, and thought it was due to our jealousy of the Mexican belles.

In January, Colonel Lane was ordered to leave Santa Fé and return to Fort Union, to command that post. His rank then was major of the Third Cavalry and brevet lieutenant-colonel.

The Third Cavalry was originally the Mounted Rifles, and I never could understand why it and the two dragoon regiments—first and second—were not allowed to retain their ancient and most honorable names, instead of calling them all "cavalry."

Colonel Charles Whiting relieved Colonel Lane at Fort Marcy, and we proceeded to Fort Union, where we found new quarters awaiting us. Their appearance was imposing, but there was no comfort in them.

The house we occupied, built for the commanding officer, consisted of eight rooms, four on each side of an unnecessarily wide hall for that dusty, windy country. They were built of adobe, and plastered inside and out, and one story high, with a deep porch in front of the house. There was not a closet nor a shelf in the house, and, until some were put up in the dining-room and kitchen, the china, as it was unpacked, was placed upon the floor. After great exertion and delay the quarter-master managed to have some plain pine shelves made for us, which, though not ornamental, answered the purpose. There was no one to have such things done but the quartermaster, no towns in the neighborhood where workmen lived and could be hired. You may be sure the quartermaster's life was a burden to him, pestered as he was from morning until night by every woman at the post, each one wanting something done, and "right away," too. But I have yet to hear of a quartermaster dying because his burdens were too heavy to bear. They are almost all hale and hearty men.

We were quite at home in a short time, and, with the addition of a young Mexican man and little Mexican girl to our establishment, we were comfortable. The man milked cows, brought wood and water, scrubbed floors, etc., besides telling the children the most marvellous tales ever invented. When a little boy he had been captured by the Indians, and, if he could have spoken English better, would have had many a bloodcurdling story to relate. The children understood his jargon better than I did, and adored him.

José (pronounced Hosay) was his name. My maid, being English, called him 'Osay. She was an endless source of amusement to him, and he tormented her beyond endurance.

The Mexican child, Haney, was a fine playmate for the children; she was good-natured, and suffered in consequence, and when the play became too rough she ran to "Mama," as she called me, to complain.

Their language was a wonderful mixture of Spanish, English, signs, and nods, but each understood it perfectly.

145

TWENTY-FIVE

COLONEL LANE, as commanding officer, seemed to feel obliged to entertain everybody who came to the post; and as our servants were inefficient and there was no market at hand, it was very difficult to have things always to please us, and, I fear, to the satisfaction of our guests.

The cook was useless half the time with rheumatism, so that I had not only all the work to do, but her to attend to besides. I took José into training when the maid was laid up, and he helped me in many ways, washing dishes, preparing vegetables for cooking, etc.

His appearance in the kitchen would have been against him in the eyes of the fastidious. His lank black hair fell over his shoulders, and he was never without his hat, but I did not interfere. I could not cultivate manners and the culinary art at the same time in a savage, and just then the latter was more important to me than the former, and I said nothing.

Early one morning I found him in the kitchen, deeply interested in preparing something for breakfast; his white shirt was outside of his trousers and hung far below his short blue jacket, which was ornamented with brass buttons. His high black felt hat was on his head as usual, and below it streamed the coarse hair. I smiled at his absurd appearance, of which he was unconscious, going steadily on with his work. I had gone into the kitchen in anything but a gay mood, with the prospect before me of cooking breakfast for a number of strange people, but at the sight of José my spirits rose.

The only cook I could find to replace my sick one was a colored woman whose right hand was deformed. I tried her, but that hand, with her lack of cleanliness, was too much for me, and I concluded I would prefer to do all the work than have her about me, and sent her off.

As the plaster dried in our new quarters the ceilings fell one by one. At least a bushel came down one night on my maid as she slept, and she nearly roused the garrison with her wild shrieks, although she was not hurt the least bit.

One day I had cooked a dinner for a family of seventeen, including children. It was on the table, and I was putting the last touches to it preparatory to retiring to the kitchen. I could not sit down with my guests and attend to matters there at the same time. I was stooping over to straighten something when I heard an ominous crack above my head, and, before I could move, down fell half the ceiling on my back and the table, filling every dish with plaster to the top. The guests had just reached the dining-room door in time to see the catastrophe, and finding I was unhurt they retired until the débris was cleared away and a second dinner prepared. Fortunately, I had plenty of food in reserve, and it was soon on the table and disposed of by my friends with apparent relish. I, in the solitude of my kitchen, could not do justice to the subject, so kept quiet.

You will see, from the foregoing, house-keeping on the frontier had its drawbacks. We had plenty to eat, such as it was, but we thought it not always dainty enough to set before our visitors. Our friends appreciated our efforts in their behalf; but we entertained many people we never had seen before and never met again. Some were so situated that they could have returned our hospitality later, but they never did, nor did they even seem aware of our existence.

We are told to take in the stranger, as by so doing we "may

entertain an angel unawares." I do not think that class of guests often travelled in Texas and New Mexico, at least while I was out there; if they did, their visits were few and far between, and their disguise was complete. My efforts to entertain an old friend at Fort Union cost me dear. I became overheated in the kitchen and had an attack of pleurisy, which left me with a cough and so weak the doctor advised me to go to Santa Fé for a rest and change. The children and cook were to go with me; the latter was better and able to work, but her exertions were not sufficient to cause a relapse. We took some bedding and the mess-chest with us, and hired rooms during our stay.

As Colonel Lane could not go with us, we left Union with a cavalry escort, stopping at a house every night. The escort of a sergeant and six or eight men were tried and trusty soldiers, in whose care we were perfectly safe, and who would have stood by us in any emergency.

After a stay of a month or six weeks in Santa Fé, I was quite well, and we returned to Fort Union. I made two visits to Santa Fé in the summer of 1867, but remained only a few days each time. It required eight days to go and return, four each way, so that a two weeks' leave from home soon passed.

The drive was always delightful to me, taken in an ambulance, with a team of four fine mules, which were quite equal to performing all the duties required of them, seeming fully to understand the necessity of making a certain number of miles daily before they could have their supper of corn and hay.

The escort rode in front at a moderate gait; the road generally was excellent, the scenery beautiful, and at times grand. The breeze, filled with the odor of pine-trees, was exhilarating and delicious,—you seemed to take in health with every breath of the pure air.

One morning our departure from the town where we passed the night was delayed. An ambulance mule was reported sick. Remedies were given him, and, as he seemed to improve, the sergeant thought he was able to travel, and for a while we bowled over the hard road at a lively rate, when, without the least warning, the poor little mule fell dead; he never stirred, seeming to die instantly. When it was found his work in this world was indeed done, it required but a few moments to cut him loose from the harness, push his body off the road, hitch up a "spike team," which means three instead of four animals, one in the lead instead of two, and start again, leaving the remains of our faithful servant to feed the coyotes and vultures, which were always at hand. The death of a mule is to me like the death of a friend, and I do not believe half the bad tales told of him.

Once, when going from Santa Fé to Fort Union, no less a person than Kit Carson—then having the rank of general— made one of the party.

To see the quiet, reticent man, you never would dream that he was the hero of so many romances. I believe he would rather have faced a whole tribe of hostile Indians than one woman, he was so diffident. But had she required assistance, he would have shed his last drop of blood in her defence.

We travelled and ate at the same table together for three or four days, and I never met a plainer, more unpretentious man in my life. One morning we were breakfasting in a room which had been occupied the night before by several very rough men. The tin basins which held water for their morning ablutions still stood about, and the scanty supply of towels adorned the chairs and tables.

We had boiled eggs for breakfast, and I asked the Mexican girl who waited upon us to bring me a cup. Without the least hesitation she took up a glass the men had used, seized one of their soiled towels, and began to polish the tumbler with it. I found my appetite had gone, and I ate no more that morning, and Kit Carson smiled quietly at my look of disgust, no doubt wondering that such a trifle could prevent one from enjoying a hearty breakfast.

I never saw him again after we reached Fort Union.

We had a pleasant garrison at Fort Union in the summer of 1867. There was a chaplain and his family, besides other charming people.

Every Sunday services were held in a room called a chapel, by the chaplain, and several ladies, I among them, made the music, which perhaps was not the finest, but was not bad.

The small melodeon I owned was sent over regularly for the use of the choir. As we wanted extra good music for Easter, we met frequently to practise, and to one chant particularly we gave much attention, singing it over and over many times. When Easter Sunday came we acquitted ourselves well, until the chant we had practised so assiduously was to be sung. While our young friend at the melodeon was playing, and it was time to begin, the soprano whispered to me that she had forgotten her part. We had no note-books, but the words were before her, and she warbled, unfalteringly, sweetest music to suit both them and the chords of the melodeon.

I followed her lead, and do not believe the congregation knew she was not singing as it was written.

She, and one other who sang that day, have long since joined the heavenly choir.

Late in the summer I spent much time making pickles and plum-jam of the wild fruit that grew abundantly in New Mexico. Delicious as they were, it was decreed we were not to eat them.

Colonel Lane's health, which had not been good, became worse, and the doctor told him he must apply for a leave and go East. It was a great surprise to us that the doctor took such a serious view of the case, but, as he said go, we obeyed.

TWENTY-SIX

WE HAD NOT been particularly comfortable at Fort Union, but we were sorry to leave. We liked the old log quarters, up towards the hills, much better than the new adobe houses, planted right down on the plain, which was swept by the winds all summer long. How they did howl! About ten o'clock every morning they woke up, and whistled and moaned, and rose to wild shrieks, doing everything wind ever does in the way of making a noise. The fine, impalpable dust worked its way into every crack and crevice, lodging round the windows and doors in little yellow mounds, so that we could sweep up a good-sized dust-pan full after the wind lulled, which it usually did at sun-down. Sometimes it blew all night, beginning with fresh vigor at the usual time next morning. Another unpleasant trick the breezes had of darting playfully down the chimney, sending the fire and ashes half-way across the room, so that we had to be on guard to prevent a conflagration.

As soon as it was decided we must leave, we made preparations for a sale of such things as we did not require for the road. My house was usually in pretty good order, but I hired a man to come daily to scrub and scour until everything shone. I was well aware how all the articles would be examined by my army sisters for spots and specks, and I was determined they should find neither.

When one of the ladies called to see me and take notes, I

was quite indignant when she whispered to me to remember how much better things sold *"when clean!"*

We had no cause to complain of the prices realized at the sale. In several instances things brought far more than they were worth. Several officers began in a joke to bid for eleven white china soup-plates, and they were knocked down to one of them for twenty-two dollars! Imagine his wife's disgust when she heard of it. All bills were paid promptly, except where some citizens, who lived a long distance off, bought a few articles, took them away, but forgot to return and settle for them.

We needed all the money we could raise for the expensive journey before us. It required a great deal to travel to and from a country as far away as New Mexico, and to have such an expense twice in one year was a serious drain on our finances.

It is almost impossible for an army officer to save money. His pay barely suffices for his monthly expenses, and he feels much gratified if after his bills are settled he has anything left over.

As a rule, he does not often run in debt, going without things for which he cannot pay. There are exceptions, of course, but I am speaking of those whom I know and officers in general. Occasionally a station is found where living is comparatively cheap, and he enjoys the prospect of putting by part of his pay in the village bank every month. But before he becomes entirely accustomed to the pleasure of being "a bloated bondholder," an order comes sending him from Maine to California, or from Oregon to Florida.

With a sigh he draws his year's savings from the bank, knowing how far short it will fall when travelling expenses are paid out of the amount and provision made for Jimmie, Margaret, baby, and nurse, not to mention Mrs. Second Lieutenant Napoleon Smith.

Poor Second Lieutenant Napoleon Smith can only hope "the Lord will provide," and he does seem to, for we almost always find the lieutenant and family there on time, however it is accomplished.

His expenses are not yet ended: the change of climate necessitates a change of clothing, and by the time each member of the family is fitted out, the exchequer is more than exhausted, and he is obliged to go in debt for a while. But the smiling members of Ketchem & Cheatham, where all the necessary purchases are made, assure the nearly demented head of the family they are always ready to give credit to army officers, and will cheerfully await his convenience to settle his bill, and there is nothing for him to do but accept their offer, much as the debt disturbs him. Then begins a system of economy and pinching until the last dollar is paid, and Second Lieutenant Napoleon Smith walks proudly away, a free man once more.

The day came at last when all was ready for us to leave Fort Union,—trunks packed and locked, the last screws put into the lids of the great wooden chests, the wagons loaded, and the ambulance at the door.

We bade our motley crowd of domestics "Adios." None were going with us. Our many kind friends came to wish us "bon voyage," and we were off.

My sixth journey across the Plains was over a new route to us, and I was glad of any variation of the scene which was so familiar to me. Our escort was small, considering the danger we ran in going through a country full of Indians, but though the party was not large, it was exceeding wary and ever on the lookout.

My eyes, from long practice, were as keen as a frontiersman's, and nothing escaped them. I saw everything unusual, near or far. A dust, a little smoke, an animal off the road, all came in for its share of investigation through the field-glass.

Next to my fear of Indians, I dreaded crossing rivers more than anything else. Some of the fords were reached by a steep and dangerous road, leading from the top of a bank to the water's edge, down which the cautious driver guided his sure-footed team. Sometimes there was a drop of a foot or two from the bank into the swift-running stream. Then I clasped my hands and shut my eyes tight, but never a sound escaped me. The children were too much absorbed with what was going on to notice me. With shouts and yells the mules were rushed through the water, men on horseback riding beside them to keep them in the track; the air was blue with the profanity thought necessary when driving mules.

The last agony was in the effort made to reach the top of the wet and slippery straight-up-and-down bank on the other side, and this feat was accomplished with even more noise than before, the shouts and cracking of whips making an appalling din.

The mules seemed to enjoy the uproar, and could hardly have done their work without it. I think they understood perfectly what was said to them, they looked so knowing and sensible: the teamsters always talked to them as if they were human, and the mule intimated he was aware of what was said and would act accordingly. Did you ever see a team in which there was not a Pete or John, Bet, Jane, or Kate?

When the ambulance stopped at the top of the opposite bank, which the mules, panting and half drowned, managed at last to reach, I opened my eyes with a feeling of gratitude that one stream, at least, had been safely crossed.

It had been decided that our best route East would be *via* Denver. The road ran through Trinidad, Pueblo, and Colorado Springs, all small settlements at that time. The scenery in

Colorado was magnificent, but it takes a more gifted pen than mine to tell of the wonderful things all around us. I was far more interested just then in avoiding Indians, and having a comfortable place where we could pass the night, than in the glories of Pike's Peak or Garden of the Gods.

We usually found a substantial log house at the end of our day's travel, where we were allowed to stay by paying for the room. It was not a "one-price" country then, for the rates charged by one man were no guide as to what we would be called upon to pay next night. We paid but fifty cents for lodgings at a very nice house, while the following day six dollars was not thought too much to ask for quarters not as good. Of course these charges were for a room and fire only,—we provided our own beds and meals.

The surroundings of the houses where we spent the nights were most picturesque,—groves of trees and gigantic rocks of singular formation were to be found everywhere, to the great delight of the children, who were tired after being shut up in the ambulance so many hours daily, and quite ready when we stopped to have a good romp before bedtime. We found them, late one evening, high up on an enormous pulpit-shaped rock, playing church.

We reached Denver in a blinding snow-storm, and drove to the best hotel in the city. No one thought it the least curious to see us arrive in a four-mule ambulance, followed by a military escort and several big wagons. As I remarked before, such sights were common out West.

After resting a day or two in Denver we started again, making for the end of the railroad, which was somewhere between Cheyenne and Julesburg. The prospect of exchanging the ambulance and tents for a Pullman car was most agreeable, especially as the weather was cold and we were liable to have snow-storms any day.

TWENTY-SEVEN

WE WERE GREATLY DISAPPOINTED when we reached Cheyenne, not to find some kind of hotel or lodging-house where we could be accommodated. Any shelter from the wintry blast would have been a luxury,—anything more substantial than a tent to keep out the bitter cold. There was every prospect of a blizzard by night, but I believe that name had not been coined then to suit the storm.

The only thing in the way of a hotel or a restaurant in the town was a long building of boards, ten or twelve feet high, surmounted by sloping rafters covered with canvas, which formed the roof. It had been used originally for a theatre, but I suppose a restaurant was more necessary, and it became an eating-house. Our tents were pitched just outside of it, when we found there was nothing better to be done. It was not until night, after the children had gone to bed, that the storm broke upon us in all its fury. The tent shook violently with the wind, and in a little while the outside was covered with a sheet of snow and ice. With all that was going on outside, you may imagine the inside was none too warm nor comfortable, and the colonel thought no better time could be found to open a bottle of fine champagne than then. It was done, and the wine poured into two tin cups, one for each. No ice was needed to cool it that night. It was the best champagne I ever tasted in my life, I think.

The storm grew worse, and it seemed as if the tent must fall upon us. The colonel determined to go again into the restaurant and ask if they could not in some way accommodate us, as it was really unsafe to remain where we were. The family occupying the building insisted it was impossible to do anything for us. Husband after that took matters into his own hands, and carried the children in, I following. As soon as I caught my breath, after my rush through the gale and sleet, I took in an amazing picture.

On what had been the stage of the theatre, with the rough scenery all about her, sat a pleasant-looking woman placidly sewing beside a bright light, and with her foot rocking a cradle in which was a young baby. She seemed perfectly at home amid the indigo-blue clouds, frowning castles, and vivid green daubs supposed to resemble trees.

When we were actually in the place there was nothing more to be said, and the woman, who did not seem at all disconcerted by our abrupt entrance, began at once to see what arrangements she could make for us.

Below the stage, and off to one side of it, was a bedstead standing on a platform just large enough to hold it. I suppose there was no floor in the building, and that is why the bed stood on a few boards. All was surrounded by canvas, painted to represent a red-brick wall, with a massive door, also painted, on the side. One bed was all they could give us; likely it was usually occupied by several members of the family. Even had we brought in our own, there was no place to put it. Some fur robes and blankets were laid under the bedstead for the children, the only spot there was.

I took the youngest with me, and the other two crawled into their uncomfortable furry nest, not the least disturbed by their peculiar resting-place. The colonel remained in the tent, on guard, all night An attempt was made to steal the mules, and had he not been on the spot it would have been successful.

We remained in the restaurant some days before leaving Cheyenne. Although the badly-built shanty was not much protection against the intensely cold weather, we could get our meals there, which was better than having to look after the cooking of them myself.

Our next move was from Cheyenne to the end of the railroad, where we parted with the escort, ambulance, etc., and took passage on a freight-train, occupying the caboose, which was to take us to Julesburg, where we would find the regular train and a Pullman car.

The night we passed in the caboose was an uneasy one. We came to a halt for hours, and I overheard a man ask another what caused the detention. His Job's comforter told him the Indians had torn up the track some miles ahead, which turned out to be untrue; but that trouble was always apprehended was apparent from the stacks of firearms on all trains.

The sight of a passenger-train was delightful, and in the sleeper we found Lieutenant John W. Bubb and wife, just from Fort Fetterman, and going East on leave. Their experiences at that extremely isolated fort were thrilling, with hostile Indians always so close it was scarcely safe to go out of doors.

We travelled to Omaha together, and no back-woodsman ever enjoyed a first car-ride more than we did the one we were then taking in the comfortable Pullman, after our late camping in the cold.

At Omaha we rested several days, Colonel Lane being quite broken down.

Mrs. Bubb and I, woman-like, went out to see the fashions, and took a look at some bonnets "just from the East, very latest styles," we were told. It had been so long since we needed a bonnet, or had seen one of the "latest," we were, of course, much interested. We took up one, but could not tell front from back. The Fanchon was worn then, and was a puzzle to an uneducated mind. After what we saw, we decided that we did not care for a bonnet until we reached home.

When Colonel Lane was better we started again. At the time of which I write there were no "buffet cars," nor even regular eating-houses on our route. Sometimes notice was given that at the next station "twenty minutes for dinner" would be allowed. We always carried our camp lunch-box with us, full of provisions, not particularly good, but well enough to quiet the pangs of hunger. We found it useless and expensive to try to take the children to a twenty-minute meal; by the time they had looked about them, it was too late to eat anything, so we gave it up. The colonel, usually, was the only one who left the cars to get a meal, but he went armed with a towel and tin coffee-pot, and, after hurrying through his dinner, brought us more provisions than we could possibly dispose of. He, poor man, never had a "square meal" when we travelled, but we could supply all deficiencies from what he provided for us.

When everything was ready for our luncheon, spread out as it was on the seats of the car, we ate it comfortably, utterly indifferent as to what other passengers thought or said. They stared at us, and no doubt took us for foreign emigrants. I dare say our appearance was singular, our clothes unfashionable, and faces weather-beaten.

We remained a year in the East, and before returning to the frontier placed our eldest daughter at school, there being no good ones in New Mexico, except the convent in Santa Fé, where we did not care to send her. So our little family circle was broken. It was dreadful to put a whole month between her and us, but it had to be done.

In November, 1868, we left for New Mexico, *via* Texas. It

was the only route practicable just then, for the Indians on the Plains were very hostile, and too late in the year, besides, to attempt to travel with children in the latitude where snow came so early.

We halted a day in Louisville, Kentucky, then took a sleeper through to New Orleans, hoping to catch a steamer for Galveston the morning after our arrival.

But no one seemed to be in a hurry but us, and several cars loaded with mules were attached to our train, in consequence of which we were nineteen hours late, and had to wait in New Orleans two days before another ship left for Texas. We stayed at the St. Charles Hotel until she sailed, when we went aboard of her, and I crossed the Gulf of Mexico for the third time.

Not being at all fond of "bounding over the glad waters of the dark blue sea," I was pleased to reach Galveston, then a pretty town of many white houses with green "blinds," the gardens filled with oleanders and orange-trees. As one of the children was indisposed, we remained several days. From Galveston to Houston we travelled by boat, and from Houston to Brenham on a wretched railroad, the only one in Texas.

We met a gentleman and his wife from Philadelphia, *en route* to San Antonio, seeking health; but they found so much discomfort at the stopping-places,—there were no "hotels,"—that they almost decided to give up the trip. But at Brenham we were able to charter a stage, so that we need not travel at night, and were more comfortable.

The roads were in a dreadful condition, as much rain had fallen recently, and it was often late at night when we stopped. The houses were so open to the winds that blew, we had to protect ourselves as well as we could from them by tacking up shawls and blankets around the beds.

At a small lodging-place we found but one room with fire. There were two beds in it, and as that was all to be had, we took one, and our friends the other. Imagine their horror when told we must share the same apartment! As it was by no means our first experience at being so situated, we were not shocked in the least. We had many a quiet laugh over the evident unhappiness of the Philadelphians at such very close quarters.

Next day, when we drove up to a house of entertainment, we found the host and his family cowering over a fire, doors open and windows broken, although it was raining and cold.

Not a place about the house had been put to rights since having been occupied the night before, and only when we arrived and wanted rooms did they make an effort to put them in order.

We were so exhausted by the time everything was ready, we had no spirit left to cavil at small discomforts.

TWENTY-EIGHT

THE FOLLOWING DAY we landed at the "Avenue Hotel," in Austin, the best there was at that time, but our room was cheerless,—no carpet, two beds, wash-stand, stove, table without a cover, and a few hide-bottom chairs. The fare was good and clean, and prices very high.

A wet norther struck the town in a day or two, and everything was flooded. The water leaked through the ceiling of our room, falling on the beds, and we were awakened in the night by the baby calling for "a rumella, 'cause it was wainin'." The storm ceased next morning, and the waters subsided, which was fortunate; the town was inundated, roads impassable from washouts, and the streets torn up by the mighty deluge that rushed through them, losing itself in the river below the town.

We met many army people stationed in Texas that winter; some of the ladies knew everything there was to be learned on matters military. They made us smile at the extent of their wisdom. I felt old fogy among them, and concluded I was the one who knew nothing. Many women spoke of *"our* regiment" and *"our* troop" (or company), as if they had command. I found I was far behind the times, believing, as I always had, that the less a woman knew of military affairs, and what went on in garrison, the better for all.

General and Mrs. Canby were there also; I had not seen them since we left Santa Fé in 1861. She was a lovely, cultivated woman, with plenty of good common sense, and admired by all.

We remained a month in Austin, waiting for news of our carriage and furniture, shipped from Philadelphia to Indianola, Texas. At the end of that time we heard the vessel had arrived, and that our goods had been sent to San Antonio. So we said good-by to our friends, and in a broken-down ambulance, with a team of four mules to correspond, we left for San Antonio. A weary, dismal drive we had for four days, through oceans of water and rivers of mud.

Perhaps some of you have ridden all day in a leaky ambulance through the cold rain, the tired mules ready to give out at any moment while making desperate efforts to pull you through mud up to the wheel-hubs. Did you like it?

The driver had no overcoat, and suffered in consequence. The colonel was too sick to assist with the mules as he usually did, so he kept the man warm internally with frequent doses of brandy, to which he did not object, nor did he once make a wry face at the medicine.

When at last we caught a glimpse of San Antonio we were much relieved, and more so when we were comfortably fixed at the Menger Hotel. It was some time before the wagon-train arrived from the coast with our property, and we had ample time to advertise for servants who would go with us to New Mexico. A colored man and woman applied for the place, and we were obliged to take them. Could we have read the future, he and she would have remained in San Antonio unto this day, as far as we were concerned.

February 3, 1869, we left San Antonio for Fort Bliss, where Colonel Lane expected to find orders assigning him to a post in New Mexico. Our route was over a part of Texas we had not travelled before. One hundred and fifteen miles from San Antonio was Fort Mason, a small but pretty post, not then garrisoned. Fort Concho came next, a new post, still unfinished. It was built on the prairie, and struck me as gloomy in the extreme. Here we were fortunate enough to meet that good fellow "Jakey Gordon," whose quarters were immediately turned over to us. They were of canvas, but larger than ordinary wall-tents, stretched over a frame, roomy and comfortable. The water at the fort was bad, and the heat in summer almost insupportable.

Between Fort Concho and Fort Stockton we crossed a part of "Llano Estacado," or "Staked Plain," inexpressibly dreary, and, but for the buffalo hunts, desolate and uninteresting; but we had plenty of excitement when the horsemen went out after the huge, awkward animals, driving them close to the road, so that we saw the chase and were almost in at the death. I preferred to be safely in the carriage when a herd of buffalo was at hand, and saw all I cared to from my coigne of vantage. After the buffalo was killed the great carcass was cut up and stowed in one of the wagons until camp was reached, when all who wanted fresh meat were supplied. To me it was tough as leather and uninviting. They told me I did not have a good piece and that I must try the hump, which was said to be very tender. I had eaten some of the hump, or attempted to do so, with no better success; the more I chewed the larger it grew. The children and colonel managed to get rid of their portion and professed to enjoy it, but my opinion never changed. The tongue was tender, but no other part that I ever tried.

The Pecos River was between us and Fort Stockton, and, on account of the quicksands, dangerous to ford. When we reached "Horsehead Crossing" one Sunday morning, it was thought safest for the children and me, and my valuable maid, to ride over in one of the wagons, as the ambulance, being comparatively light, was likely to upset or float down stream, either of which would have been disagreeable. Ropes were tied to the wheels and held by mounted men, but even then it rolled from side to side, so that I did not care to look at it until it was safely on the other bank.

The sheet on one of the heavy wagons was thrown back, and we mounted to the top of the load. The colonel disposed of all surplus clothing and his boots, taking up a position on the tongue of the wagon, to be ready in case of emergency.

Then came the plunge into the treacherous, rapid stream, and the wagon trembled and careened as it struck the quicksands. The teamsters coaxed and scolded, urged and swore at the mules, to prevent them stopping short of the opposite side of the river. I shut my eyes, and ears too. In the same team some of the mules were almost out of the water while others were nearly under it, caused by the quicksand shifting and changing position, thus making the crossing unsafe.

I could not help thinking what a sight we should have been that beautiful Sunday morning to our Eastern friends, then quietly seated in church, if they could have watched us fording the Pecos River. If they had not known who we were, they would never have recognized us, dressed for camping, and riding emigrant fashion, in a wagon.

We were seven days going from Fort Concho to Fort Stockton, where we arrived cold and tired. Colonel and Mrs. Wade came to our relief, and entertained us while we stayed at the post.

One day a pet prairie-dog attacked Mrs. Wade's young baby during the absence of the family from the room: it climbed up on the bed and scratched the little face and head. The child's cries brought the mother and everybody from the dining-table, and there sat the small animal by the baby, tearing the tender flesh with its needle-like claws. It had never seemed vicious before, and never had an opportunity to be so again.

Fort Stockton had improved wonderfully since my sister and I did our washing there, on a Sunday morning, ten years before, but I did not care to stay long.

At Fort Davis we remained a day, to rest and put everything in order. Our man, the incomparable colored one who came with us from San Antonio, took that opportunity to clean and load his revolver, when, without warning, it went off, cutting a hole in the felt hat he wore. If the ball had stopped short of the hat it might have been bad for William, but the world would have had one rascal the less. There was a heavy snowstorm that day, which made camp more than unpleasant.

In the Limpia Cañon, or Wild Rose Pass, in the vicinity of Fort Davis, there was some beautiful scenery. I cannot now remember just how far from the fort this dangerous pass was, but it had always been a noted hiding-place for Indians, and many a careless traveller had cause to repent his lack of vigilance while going through it. Indeed, the whole road from Limpia Cañon to Fort Quitman had been the scene of repeated tragedies. Only a month before we passed over it, the stage, carrying a passenger and the United States mail, had been attacked by Indians, the driver killed, and Judge Hubbell, a man well known in Texas and New Mexico, either murdered or captured; the mail was cut to pieces and the coach destroyed. A wooden cross, with his name upon it, marked the spot where the body of the driver was found. The date "January, 1869," was also cut upon the cross.

It made me shudder to think what a short time had elapsed since that desperate, hopeless struggle took place, two brave men fighting for life against an unknown number of devils.

I was riding in the buggy one day when the guard came up to report that a number of Indians had been seen not far away. I was ordered into the ambulance, and hasty preparations were made to give them a proper reception, should they attempt to attack us; but they, like ourselves, perhaps, assumed the defensive, rather than the aggressive. The Indian rarely made war unless certain of victory, which he followed up with untold atrocities.

TWENTY-NINE

On THE DAY the Indians were seen we were to reach Eagle Spring, a spot where many bloody battles had been fought between white men and Indians. It was the usual campground, as no water was found again until we reached the Rio Grande, thirty miles away.

The spring was some distance up a gorge, at the foot of a mountain; the ground was rough and rocky, so that any number of Indians could hide until an opportunity arrived to make an attack. Small parties camped on the plain, beside the road, and, with sentinels out to keep watch, drove the animals to the spring for water and then back to camp.

Our horses and mules were watered, then hitched up and driven ten miles farther, when a dry camp was made for the night, thus taking ten miles off our next day's march of thirty miles to the Rio Grande. It was very late, and all were busy in various ways, and preparations were made to secure the camp against any attack the Indians might make.

The mules were turned out for what grazing they could find before being fastened to the wagons for the night. After a while it was discovered that they with the herders and sentinels were getting too far from camp, and orders were sent for them to come in at once.

When our tents were in order we called the children, who had a few moments before been playing close by. Only one responded; the boy was nowhere to be seen. For a little while there was great consternation; the camp was searched, but without avail; it began to look as if he had been spirited away in the darkness. Just when the excitement was becoming too intense to bear, the mules were driven in, and there, sitting in front of one of the herders, with a great whip in his hand, was the child, radiantly happy, and evidently believing he had charge of the herd. But there were no more expeditions of that kind made without our express permission. A little child in camp or garrison could always do as it pleased with the men, no matter how rough the latter might be. Had anything happened to that baby boy, every man there would have given his life for the child.

When we sighted the Rio Grande, five miles below Fort Quitman, a sense of relief took the place of my recent uneasiness and fear; and when we drove into the forlorn and tumbledown adobe-built fort, I wanted to greet everybody as a friend and brother. The troops stationed there were colored, and as we passed the guard-house I noticed a sergeant in full dress, jumping rope! I felt rather shocked to see a soldier in uniform so disporting himself, but concluded if any one at Quitman could feel cheerful enough to enjoy so innocent a pastime he was to be congratulated.

From Quitman to Fort Bliss the journey was comparatively a safe one. There were several Mexican settlements, and the wretched huts were objects of interest, especially when their occupants turned out to look at us; the life about the villages, still as it was, was pleasant. We had not seen a living thing, except at the garrisons through which we passed, beyond a prairie-dog or an occasional crow and some Indians in the distance, since we left the Staked Plains, where vast herds of buffalo were grazing on every side, happy in their freedom and roaming over the unsettled country for hundreds of miles.

It seemed to me I knew every stone and bush on the lonely

road from Fort Davis to the Rio Grande, and I think even yet
I would remember some of them.

It would be a pleasure to me to travel that route now in a
palace car on the railroad, dashing over those dreary camp-
grounds, with whistles shrieking and headlights blazing, wak-
ing the echoes and illuminating the country far and wide. For
when we travelled with small parties we were afraid to speak
loud, or have a fire or light, lest we attract the attention of the
Indians, never far away.

That time has gone forever, and those tedious marches
need not be made again. I always enjoyed them when our escort was sufficiently large to give a feeling of perfect security,
but more often than not they were too small, and the risks we
ran were very great, but there seemed to be no help for it, and
I suffered mentally in consequence. You will think I was a
dreadful coward; but put yourself in my place, you woman,
and would you have felt any braver than I did? When brought
face to face with danger, as I have been on more than one occasion, I flatter myself I behaved pretty well, being outwardly,
at least, very cool and quiet. What I felt need not be mentioned here.

The Fort Bliss of 1869 was not the one we knew and enjoyed so much. Great inroads had been made by the Rio
Grande: some of the buildings were washed away, so that the
old post was abandoned, and the garrison moved to quarters a
mile away. Our old house still stood, but the roof had fallen in.
The others were masses of crumbling adobe. What changes
had taken place since we were all so happy there a few years
before!

We remained a day or two at Bliss, until Colonel Lane's
orders were received, to proceed to Fort Selden, New Mexico,
and take command. It was a new post, since the war, not far
from Fort Fillmore.

We had been thirty-four days on the road from San Antonio to Fort Bliss, but we only travelled twenty-nine of them; the other five were spent at the forts *en route*, for rest, repairs, etc.

On our way to Fort Selden we passed within sight of old Fort Fillmore. As far as we could discover, the adobe quarters had returned to the dust of which they were made; not one house was left standing.

Our new station was a quiet, rather unattractive place, garrisoned by one company of colored infantry and one of white cavalry. The commanding officer's quarters were not nearly finished. I believe there were only four rooms ready when we arrived, but they were larger and better than a tent, and we were not long in getting into them. The house was square, built of adobe, with, if I remember aright, four rooms on each side of a wide hall. Our porch was of brush laid across poles, and supported by the same,—a fine harbor for snakes, scorpions, and such things, but they did not annoy us much. There were four ladies there, none of whom are now in the army. They were not friendly with each other, but I, coming as a stranger among them, was kindly received, and we lived most harmoniously together as long as we remained. It was, indeed, a dull little place.

We owned horses, mules, and vehicles of various kinds, but on account of Indians it was unsafe to ride a mile from the post; and when we drove as far as we dared go, there was always a loaded revolver in the carriage. We rode a good deal, notwithstanding, in our light buggy, with a horse that could outrun any that an Indian was likely to own.

That summer I determined to make butter and raise chickens, and I succeeded remarkably well, considering all things. I do not believe the famous butter-makers of Pennsylvania could have done any better than I did under the circumstances.

There was no ice, remember, and no cool, sparkling spring at hand. I took care of the milk myself, saving all the cream I could spare for the butter. The cows were not the best, but good for that country. My churn was primitive,—only a large stone jar, which held about three gallons. A soldier-carpenter made the top and dasher of pine wood, and a rough job it was.

The water we used at Fort Selden was brought fresh every morning from the muddy Rio Grande, and emptied into barrels kept for the purpose. It was of the color of rich chocolate. To settle enough for drinking, it was poured into large, porous earthen jars, holding several gallons each. By degrees the impurities sank to the bottom of the jar, and the water oozed through it, keeping the contents quite cool.

Ours were covered with pieces of blanket which retained the moisture, and they were placed on a bench in which holes were cut for the purpose of holding them. This bench was kept in the shadiest, coolest spot to be found; but the weather at Selden was very hot, so that the water was not often what one would desire. It was the best we had, though, to wash and cool the butter, which sometimes was like oil when freshly churned. Frequently I found it impossible to separate the butter and milk. I would then put the jar aside for the night, and next day in the cool of the morning I finished my dairy work.

Years ago I heard that all the butter procurable at army posts in Arizona had to be poured from a bottle, so it seems people there were worse off than we were in New Mexico, and had fewer advantages.

In about four months, under many difficulties, I made about one hundred and fifty pounds of butter, a good deal of which I packed down for future use.

The man and woman we took with us from San Antonio were worthless; it seems there had been some love-making between them, and the opportunity offered them by us to see the world and visit pastures new was not to be despised. Before we reached Selden the man was discharged for theft, and the maid might have been sent off for the same reason, but there was not another woman to be hired, so I was obliged to keep her. She was amiable, if she did break more than one of the commandments. We were obliged to overlook many vagaries and eccentricities of deportment, if we hoped to keep a maid on the frontier at that time. A woman of any kind was thought better than none.

THIRTY

WHEN TRAVELLING ALONG the road below Fort Davis, a white man, mounted on the smallest of ponies, joined us, after asking permission to do so. He was a bright fellow, and we allowed him to stay about the tents, feeding him for what he did, and he was always working at something.

When the colored man was discharged we put the stranger, Isaac Bloomfield, in his place, and an excellent hand he proved to be at almost everything. He was an Englishman, and had been in the English navy, where, he told me, he "got more kicks than ha'-pence."

When we could no longer close our eyes to the delinquencies of our maid, we told her we had no further use for her valuable services, and she left; so Isaac was installed as cook. He did all the housework, except making the beds; if I had permitted it, he would have done that too. The children were devoted to him, and he to them. He was quite a good plain cook; perhaps I was not very critical, infinitely preferring his cooking to my own.

One of my pastimes on the frontier was the care of chickens, gathering the eggs, setting hens, etc. I went many times a day into the coop to look at and talk to my favorites.

Before the maid left us she heard a great commotion one night in the chicken-house; though lacking in sundry virtues, she was courageous, apparently, for she went unattended to find out the cause of the disturbance. On opening the door she was startled to see a small coyote killing the chickens right and left. She ran into the house to tell the colonel, who, armed with his revolver, went with her, she going ahead, holding the candle aloft. They bearded the lion in his den; in other words, the coyote in the chicken-coop. Mary was more afraid of the report of the pistol than of the wolf. She jumped at every shot, almost dropping the light in her excitement.

It took but a few seconds to dispose of the wretched beast. Mad with hunger, he had crawled through a small opening in the main door of the coop which I had forgotten to shut that night. He killed a number of my setting-hens, they being in nests close to the ground, while the others, roosting high, were out of reach. When discovered he had not begun his feast, but was making ready with a liberal hand. It hurt my feelings to see so many of my precious chickens dead; but as their destroyer was dead, too, I was somewhat consoled.

Our table was well supplied with eggs and the chickens I raised, but it was always a difficult matter to kill them, the children begging that the life of this pretty white hen or that beautiful red rooster might be spared; the only way was to have it done without their knowledge.

As the summer went by, the rooms in the house were finished one by one, so that we had a place to put any visitors who came that way; but they did not seem to have much business at Selden, for I only remember having two guests, Colonels Bridgeman and Cary, paymasters.

I never objected to entertaining men; they were easily pleased, and willing to make due allowance for lack of variety of dainties in the larder. I must confess to a feeling of uneasiness when the wives came too, lest they might not be satisfied with our very plain style of housekeeping. We had very little furniture, and those things which the quartermaster could not supply we tried to make ourselves, or used something that answered the same purpose. For instance, one of our washstands was made of a small hogshead, in which some china had been packed. It was turned upside down, and round it I tacked a white muslin drapery; then, with a large towel spread over the top, the effect was good, especially when the pretty toilet articles were placed upon it. We made a table in the same way, and this kind of simplicity answered for ourselves, but I think some of the lady visitors might not have been quite pleased with such primitive arrangements.

At the end of four months, the colonel's health failed so rapidly the doctor told him he must not only leave Fort Selden, but New Mexico, and he must lose no time in going.

We arranged our affairs to start immediately, and had an auction of the furniture, etc., we did not care to keep; in fact, we retained only such things as were absolutely necessary. The high prices realized at our sale were absurd, and I was actually ashamed when articles were bid up far beyond their value. Our cook-stove, which cost us about forty-five dollars, sold for eighty. My sewing-machine, for which I paid less than forty, brought one hundred dollars, and everything went at the same rate. A large tin can, which was full of lard when we left San Antonio, had a few pounds still in it, and it sold for more than the original cost. You see those were the days when freight was carried from the States in wagons, and sent all over New Mexico; and the cost of transportation, added to the price of the article you wished to purchase, made it very expensive, so that what was paid to us was much less than the merchants would have charged for the same thing. Our freight was taken from the coast to New Mexico in government wagons, so that it cost us no more than the original price and the transportation from Philadelphia to Texas by sea.

After Isaac became our cook we bought his pony. It was sold also, and as it brought more than we paid for it, we divided the surplus with him, which pleased him greatly.

We were much relieved to find that we not only had not lost by our auction, but made money; and, as another expensive expedition was before us, we were glad to have enough for our wants. We had just begun to recover financially from our last journey to New Mexico, *via* Texas, and if our sale had failed to supply part of the sum required for the one about to be taken, we would have been forced to borrow money to pay expenses. To have a debt hanging over us long would have driven me insane, I believe.

I think only two officers who were at Fort Selden at that time are now in the army, Captains Russell and Elting. Dr. Seguin, one of the physicians stationed there, is now living in New York, and very eminent and skillful. I suppose he has forgotten the experiments he delighted to make with toads and ravens, feeding deadly poisons to them, some of which had no effect whatever. Selden was a fine field for one who desired to test the efficacy of certain drugs on toads, for the place was swarming with them, so that I disliked going out of doors at night, at which time they took possession of every walk and road about the place. You were sure, almost, if you stepped outside your door, to feel a soft, wriggling mass under your foot. With a screech you jumped to the other side, only to land on a second toad; by that time you were ready to go home.

One beautiful July morning we drove away from Fort Selden with not one pang of regret, and dry-eyed. We were bound for Santa Fé, and our faithful Isaac was with us, as overseer in general and in charge of the culinary department in particular. There was sorrow in our first camp. Our beautiful buggy horse fell sick, and died in a few hours. The tears we failed to shed that morning when leaving Selden flowed freely for him at night.

Science and human energy had wrought a wonderful

change in the "Jornado del Muerto" since we made that anxious and exciting night march across it in July, 1861.

About in the centre of it an artesian well had been sunk, and an abundance of good water was the result. A comfortable ranch was built, with a high stockade about it for protection, and strangers who desired to remain were given accommodations. It was really an oasis in the desert. All government animals and employés used the water without charge, but it was sold to citizen travellers.

We drove along the old familiar road without incident or accident, except the upsetting of one of the wagons while going down a very steep hill. I was perfectly unmoved when I saw it turn a somersault, knowing there was nothing in it that could be injured. All the good china and small amount of furniture we had was disposed of before leaving Fort Selden, and there was nothing in our mess-chest but tin plates, cups without handles, dilapidated saucers, and dishes to match.

One evening we camped on a high bluff, not far from a Pueblo or Indian village. The inhabitants were peaceful, law-abiding citizens, who as yet had not adopted the conventional evening-dress. Our camp in their immediate neighborhood was as good as a circus to them; they fairly crowded about the tents, where preparations for supper were going on, which they watched with intense interest.

Biscuit-dough was made up, cut out, and ready to be baked, coffee ground, etc.

The air was hot; storm-clouds lowered in the sky; the Indians wore heavy blankets, at which I wondered, but I was only a short time finding out there was not a vestige of clothing beneath them. While watching everything intently, the wearers were overcome with the heat, and away went the blankets until they cooled off sufficiently to replace them.

Soon the wind began to blow in little ominous puffs, and

the board with the unbaked biscuit upon it was carried into the tent, while all the articles lying around were hastily gathered up and put in a safe place,—none too soon, for the storm burst upon us suddenly, scattering the light red dust over everything inside and outside of the tent, ornamenting our pretty white unbaked biscuit with a coating of the finest red sand.

My uninvited guests left hurriedly to seek shelter from the abundant showers that fell, and we were glad to have them go, though the cause of their hasty departure deprived us of our supper that night. Everything prepared was ruined, and had to be thrown away, so that we had nothing but stale bread to eat, which at least kept us from starving.

THIRTY-ONE

As THERE WERE several Mexican and Indian settlements along the Rio Grande, the journey was much less tiresome than many we had made, where for hundreds of miles there was not a house to be seen in early days.

Socorro was one of the towns through which we passed, and where we had stopped at the house of an American living there very comfortably.

I remember an incident that happened once when going down the country. Some miles before we reached Socorro, the road ran over what was called the "Sand-Hills," where the travelling was slow and difficult, and the wagons fell behind the ambulance some little distance.

I was riding with the colonel in the buggy, when our attention was attracted to the manœuvres of some men on ponies, who were circling round and round on the low sand-hills, about six hundred yards to the right of us. There were, I suppose, twelve in all, and in true Indian fashion they wrapped their blankets about their bodies in thick folds before dashing up the road to meet us. Every one was certain they were Navajos from their actions. When I went back into the ambulance the driver assured me *"Them was* Navajos, because he had just been in their country and *knowed 'em,"* and he took his rifle in hand for business. The two or three soldiers with us had their rifles ready and cocked. The colonel was on the ground by the head of the horse, with his arm through the bridle and a revolver in his hand. For a few moments the suspense was awful;

no one in the ambulance spoke, as we watched the supposed Indians galloping, with arms and legs working, to the top of the hill.

When they saw our warlike attitude they shouted "Amigos" (friends), and affected much surprise that they were mistaken for Indians. They were "Mexicanos," and meant no harm,—so they said. Probably, if they had not found us as well prepared as we were to receive them, they would have attacked us for plunder or murder, as the case might be.

When the matter was mentioned to the American in Socorro, he was very indignant, and said it had been done intentionally; that the escort should have fired upon them, as they undoubtedly had designs upon us.

So you see I was always anxious when travelling with small parties, and I am certain I had enough of "sudden fears" to turn my hair gray in a "single night;" but in my case something more was required, for it has not changed color to this day, although I have had shocks sufficient to ruin my nervous system and whiten my locks.

On another occasion we were going from Santa Fé to Fort Union, when we came to a place where the road forked. Just at that point was a burro (or donkey), seemingly just killed. I wondered that it should be lying there, but could get no explanation from the colonel, or the escort, how it came to be dead on the road, although they knew all the circumstances from a traveller whom we had met. He said a party of Indians had crossed the road a little while before, and meeting a Mexican, murdered him and killed the burro, leaving its body on the spot to show others what might be their fate. I do not know what had been done with the body of the man; we only saw the little dead burro. Every one was on the watch, until we were miles away from the place where the poor wretch had been murdered; then I was told of it.

When we reached Santa Fé in the summer of 1869, we obtained permission to occupy some empty quarters at Fort Marcy, where we decided to remain for a few months. The weather was perfect,—very different from that we had left at Fort Selden.

Our scant allowance of furniture was arranged in the rooms in a few moments, and assuredly did not strike our visitors as being luxurious. Many no doubt thought we were not even comfortable, but were quite content and very happy, although our only carpet was an old tent-fly, our beds four cots, making the room look like a ward in the hospital, Dr. Huntington said. At the window I tacked up a red army blanket for a curtain, and with two or three camp chairs you have the contents of the apartment.

Army people were not surprised at the meagre display of adornment, but I thought civilians were rather startled; however, I took no trouble to explain, nor to apologize for appearances. I was not afraid of robbers, having nothing anybody would carry off. Our quarters were left to the mercy of any one who chose to enter. Isaac still presided in the kitchen, and kept the house in good order.

Early in the fall (I believe it was), Annie, daughter of General Getty, U.S.A. was married to Charles McClure, U.S.A. The wedding was as brilliant as it was possible to have it at that time; there was no railroad to bring flowers and dainties from "the States;" but the supper was very handsome and everybody was there to enjoy it.

In 1869 we found the mail facilities much improved since our former visits to Santa Fé. There was a daily stage running to and from the end of the railroad then being built towards New Mexico, a wonderful change from the monthly mail of yore. While on the frontier we received a great deal of our clothing through the mails, as express charges were very high, often amounting to more than the cost of the article received.

When we were stationed at Fort Union I ordered a melodeon from Philadelphia, and on the box was marked distinctly, "to be sent by first *wagon-train* from Fort Riley, Kansas, to Fort Union, New Mexico." By some blunder it was sent out on the stage as express matter, and the charges were "fifty-three dollars." The melodeon cost fifty.

The pleasure it gave me more than compensated for the large amount paid for getting it out. There was not then a piano at the post, and, although a melodeon is a mournful, grunty, wheezy instrument, a cross between an accordion and an indifferent organ, it was much better than nothing.

When we left New Mexico it was bought from us for *one hundred dollars*, to be used in a Protestant church in Santa Fé, then struggling for a foothold, which it secured at last, after great perseverance. In it there is now a good organ. What has become of the melodeon since the advent of its more pretentious relation, I never heard.

There were many pleasant army families in Santa Fé between the years 1866 and 1869. These, with the citizens, made a large circle of refined and cultivated people. Among them were Governor and Mrs. Mitchell, Judge and Mrs. Slough, Judge and Mrs. Houghton, General Getty and family, Colonel and Mrs. A. B. Carey, Colonel and Mrs. Bridgman, Major Rucker, the Rochesters, Kobbès, Bells, Watts, Dr. Huntington and wife, Dr. McKee, Charles McClure and wife, Mr. and Mrs. Griffin, Mr. and Mrs. Elkins, Mr. and Mrs. Edgar, and many others whose names I cannot now recall. Altogether we had a charming society.

I have scarcely more than mentioned that most important beast of burden in New Mexico,—the burro, or donkey. No load is too heavy nor awkward for him to carry, it seems. Wood was brought from the hills to the towns, cut and ready for the fire, fastened on his back and sides by raw-hide thongs. He was loaded down with masses of fodder, which left nothing to be seen of him but eyes, ears, and hoofs. Indeed, there was nothing to be transported that a Mexican did not strap to a burro; very frequently two men rode the same little beast, guiding him by punches in the head and neck with a sharp stick.

Nothing caused such agonizing fear in a mule as the sight of a loaded burro; they did not recognize each other as brothers. Sometimes, when riding quietly along the road, we would come suddenly upon a drove of burros with their packs; instantly the mules were terror-stricken, trying to push to the side of the road, or even to turn round,—anything to get away from those moving masses, the locomotive power of which they could not understand; even the sight of the burro himself was not reassuring. It was a happy day for the children when wood was brought to the house on a burro. He was driven into the corral, where, by a dexterous pull at a rawhide string, his load fell to the ground, and the patient little animal was relieved for a moment. But as soon as the wood was off his back the children were on it, and round and round they rode as long as the polite, lazy Mexican would stay, and he never seemed to be in a hurry. The burro's feelings were not consulted; his labors were arduous, his pleasures few. Six years ago the burro was still carrying the same heavy loads as of old, in Santa Fé, droves of them appearing in the narrow streets, closely followed by their owners, Mexicans and Indians, who seemed to have a wonderful faculty for keeping them in the path. Did one wander to the right or left, tempted by the sight of a morsel of paper or handful of shavings, off of which he hoped to lunch, he was soon made aware of his indiscretion by a punch from the sharp stick, and a vigorous "Shoo!" from his master, when he would again meekly join his companions, fully convinced of the folly, on his part, of trying to enjoy himself even in a mild way.

As the fall advanced we decided to push on to Fort Union, where we were to make final preparations to cross the Northern Plains for the seventh time. When our trunks and mess-chest were packed and beds rolled up we were ready to start, and I said farewell to Santa Fé, not dreaming of seeing it and "Old Baldy's" hoary head ever again, but we have been to the ancient city several times since.

We remained at Fort Union some days. Before we left we were serenaded by the band of the Third Cavalry, formerly Mounted Rifles.

After the music was over the soldiers drank to the health of their old officer and, as they expressed it, "his lady."

The weather was delightful for travelling, though the nights were more than cool. Just as soon as Colonel Lane was well enough to go we were off.

We remained a night and part of a day at Maxwell's Ranch in the Ute country, the Indians coming and going about the house, evidently without restriction, so that they did not hesitate to walk right into our room when they saw the door open. One of them, a great tall chief, I offended mortally; with majestic mien he strode into the house, rolled in his blanket and wearing on his head a tall black felt hat with a feather in it. After he had shaken hands with the colonel,—but taking no notice of me whatever,—I walked up to him and said, "Soldier," in Spanish. Staring at me with the utmost scorn, he sailed out of the room without a word. Whether he did not like to be called a soldier, or was indignant that a white squaw had spoken to him, I could not tell, but he did not return.

A round piece of tin cut from a tomato-can, and thrown out of doors, afforded the greatest satisfaction to the fortunate finder, and he and a friend gravely discussed the question as to where it would show to best advantage, on scalp-lock, necklace, or bracelet.

At Trinidad we found quite a village had sprung up, and a small tavern, where travellers were entertained. Like all new far Western towns, its reputation was most unsavory, and it was a question whether to stay in the house and run the risk of being robbed and murdered, or camp in the cold away from the town. We concluded we liked the shelter of four stout walls more than the airy ones of the tent, and went to the tavern.

Every man you met wore, as a matter of course, a revolver and knife to be ready for all emergencies, quarrels being frequently brought about for the mere pleasure of fighting. One of the first things that struck me always when we reached civilization was the absence of the belt from a man's waist, in which he carried all kinds of weapons; we were so accustomed to the sight on the frontier, I missed it. It was pleasant, though, to feel one might go half a mile from his home without running the risk of being murdered, and that it was not necessary to be always armed.

THIRTY-TWO

OUR ROAD RAN through (or near) Fort Lyon, Colorado, where we spent a day at Colonel W. H. Penrose's pleasant home, and enjoyed the change and rest.

At our first halting-place after leaving that post we were overtaken by Captain Yates and his troop of Seventh Cavalry. We stayed all night at the small board shanty used as a mail-station, occupying the state apartment, I suppose, for the walls were papered with illustrations from various pictorials. I had a suspicion the pictures were put there more to keep out the wind—of which there is an undue allowance of kind and quality in Colorado—than to embellish the room. A bright and cheery little place it was, with windows that commanded a view of the country for miles in every direction, and the road along which travelled those brave cavalrymen with their much-loved captain at the head of the column. They were going our way for several days, and we were glad of the addition to our small escort, and sorry when the time came to separate. I never met Captain Yates again. He and his gallant soldiers were massacred with Custer and his command, none returning to tell the tale.

From Fort Lyon we travelled through a part of the country we had never seen before to Fort Wallace, of which post we had heard frequently, and generally disagreeably.

A friend I had known well at Fort Union, New Mexico, and for whom I had a most tender regard, died of cholera at Fort Wallace, while on her way to New York. The fearful disease broke out among the soldiers going East; she went about doing everything in her power to relieve the sick, until she became a victim herself, and died in a short time. She was the wife of Colonel Henry Bankhead, U.S.A., and a daughter of the late Bishop Wainright, of New York.

Her heart was light when she left us at Fort Union at the prospect of so soon seeing her home and friends. In a few weeks came the news that she had died in a tent at (or not far from) Fort Wallace.

So my ideas of the place were not pleasant, and were unchanged when we saw it. The kindness extended to us by Major Butler and wife, of an infantry regiment, we cannot forget, they taking care of us all most hospitably. We were sorry that he and his family were obliged to live at such a dreary frontier post.

When we left Fort Wallace we went as straight as we could travel to the end of the railroad, where we found a small settlement named after a big man,—Sheridan. The hotel was a good-sized weather-board shell, in which were two stories of stalls called "rooms." The partitions were only seven or eight feet high, and privacy was out of the question. Had "Peeping Tom" been there, he could have plied his trade and satisfied his curiosity without any attempt at secrecy, the cracks in the boards being wide enough to admit the boldest stare.

Our "stall" was quite large, having two beds in it, but the supply of water for bathing purposes was extremely limited; a quart pitcher would have held all which we found in the room, and which we used recklessly, calling loudly for "more water." We were told we could have no more until next day, the spring being a great distance from the house. As we were to leave the following morning, we wondered where the water was to come from for our early ablutions. It was soon made clear to us, if we were so very particular as to require water every day, we must use over again that which we were about to discard; so I placed the basin with the soap-suds in it on the floor for safe-keeping. When retiring, I put my shoes and stockings not far away from the precious water. By some means it was upset, and the only foot-covering I had at hand was saturated. The colonel, having caused the disaster, meekly gathered everything up, repaired to the hotel parlor, and dried them before the fire, regardless of the assembled guests. It was useless in that house to try to do anything secretly. The sounds from bar-room and kitchen, not to mention odors, were distinctly audible and apparent in every part of the establishment, and an odd mixture of conversation reached us from the rooms around us.

Dr. Alexander, U.S.A., and family were at the hotel that same night,—they on their way to New Mexico, we going East.

What a pleasure it was to be on a train of cars and hear the conductor shout to the tardy ones, "All aboard!" and to feel ourselves rattling over the country to Kansas City. We did not realize that when we reached Sheridan the old army-life for us was ended. Had I known, I would have lingered fondly about our last camp and have said good-by to the faithful, sturdy little mules that had brought us so safely over many weary miles.

Our last long march began at Fort Selden, New Mexico, and ended at Sheridan, Kansas. We went East, fully expecting to return to the frontier in a few months, but it was not to be.

At Kansas City we parted with our faithful Isaac, to the deep distress of the children. He secured a situation from the quartermaster at Fort Leavenworth, and passed out of our knowledge.

Our daughter, whom we had left at school, waited anxiously for our arrival, and we were happy to be all together once more.

As I mentioned before, we never returned to our old frontier life again. We have been in New Mexico, California, and Texas several times since, but only as visitors. Colonel Lane was retired from active service in 1870, to my great grief.

It seemed impossible at the time that I could ever settle down to quiet, civilized, respectable life, and remain in the same place year after year. I had become so accustomed to change station every few months, I liked it, and was always ready and glad to go when an order came to move. We had never lived more than six months at one post, and three or four in the same place gave us the feeling of old inhabitants. We made nine moves in eighteen months in New Mexico, and I did not object at all. I soon fell into the habit of putting very few tacks in curtains and carpets, so that but little force was required to haul down one and pull up the other, and in a short time everything was packed and ready for a march.

Such rapid preparations cannot be made now-a-days, nor is there any necessity for it, as there was years ago. Time is required to dismantle and break up the beautiful home even the youngest lieutenant now occupies. Professional packers are needed to insure the safe transportation of the lovely glass, china, and exquisite pictures found in so many army quarters to-day. Then, when everything is ready, it is stowed away in a freight-car, chartered most probably by the said lieutenant at his own expense, to carry his "traps" to a new station.

Army quarters are better, distance is annihilated by steam, transportation is excellent, even to remote stations; but yet, with all these advantages and so-called modern improvements, are army officers and their families happier than those of thirty or more years ago? I tell you, nay!

I was much impressed at the time of the late Sioux outbreak with the contrast between an old-time "scout" and the modern way of going to war with Indians. *Our* heroes mounted their horses and away they rode into the wilderness, to be gone for weeks or months, as the case might be, while all the news we had of them was brought by a guide or soldier, mounted on a swift horse, and who very often risked his life to bring news to the post. This mode of carrying despatches was called an "express." Imagine the excitement when we heard "an express" from the scout had arrived. We did not dare to think how long a time had elapsed since the man had left it with his letters, private and official, and what might be the fate of the party since his departure.

All this is changed now, and an Indian war is carried on differently. The troops and horses are loaded on steam-cars, howitzers and ammunition sent to "the front" in the same way, while the telegraph is in constant operation noting the arrival and departure of regiments, asking for supplies, and sending the news of the last brush with the enemy far and wide over the land. And, strangest of all, the ladies at one of the posts in Nebraska, by going to a village three miles away, could actually talk to their husbands, then at the seat of war, through the telephone! This seemed to bring the matter right into their own homes. It was something I could scarcely believe or understand, this fighting Indians with all the modern improvements, so different from the old slow way. And the savages, too, have changed somewhat their methods of warfare.

The scions of the various tribes have been educated by the government and well drilled in military tactics at schools in the East, so that when they return to the tepees in the far West they are quite capable of teaching the ways of the white man to their fathers and brothers, and the proper and most advantageous use of their guns of newest pattern.

THIRTY-THREE

Y EARS HAVE PASSED since the events in this simple history occurred; many more have been forgotten. No notes nor journal of much importance were ever kept of our wanderings, which in after-years we regretted exceedingly. In the roving life we led, travelling at least eight thousand miles in an ambulance, we saw much that was novel and interesting, had thrilling adventures frequently, but I cannot recall them with sufficient distinctness to tell of them, and, besides, your patience must now be waning, after following me thus far in these reminiscences of old army days.

My experience was that of hundreds of other women, many of whom are far more capable than I of telling the story; but few, if any, have done it, and only the younger ones, with no knowledge of ante-bellum days.

Our daughters have followed in the footsteps of grandmother and mother, and married army officers,—cavalry officers.

The relics of our "old army" days are few now; but occasionally in unpacking our chests and trunks, stowed away in a garret, I find something that brings by-gone years vividly before me; it may be a tarnished shoulder-strap, a spur, or a big knife in its leather sheath; each has its history, and I dream while holding them in my hand; the lapse of time is forgotten. I am young again, wandering through the old familiar scenes.

Not long ago I came across the battered tin box in which our daily luncheon was carried when travelling from camp to camp. The paint was worn off the top, reminding me of a hoary-headed veteran, "grown gray in the service."

As I raised the lid a faint odor seemed to rise from its depths, and in a second memory was busy with the past, travelling back to the old happy days when the little tired, hungry children with eager out-stretched hands stood by my side waiting to be served. With a sigh I closed the box, putting it aside as worthless, to be thrown away, but the tender recollections awakened by the sight of the old friend were too strong. Hurriedly seizing it, I cleared a comfortable corner in a chest and carefully replaced the worn-out box, retiring it, like an old soldier, from active service forever!

And, lest you weary of this o'er-true tale, I will "retire" too.

THE END

Ger. Dawon =   p. 32
Dhanis - Ger. settlement. p. 73